# SEX WAS GOD'S IDEA

## An Honest Look at Biblical Sexuality
## And the Rightful Role of Women

# DEAN ROBERTSON

ISBN 979-8-88540-756-4 (paperback)
ISBN 979-8-88540-757-1 (digital)



Christian Faith Publishing
832 Park Avenue
Meadville, PA 16335
www.christianfaithpublishing.com

All pictures and images are provided by 123RF Stock Photography Company and are used with their permission.

Printed in the United States of America

# CONTENTS

By far the biggest factor propelling women out of the church is sex. The #churchtoo movement attested to just how damaging irresponsible handling of the church's message of sexual purity can be for some women.

—Katie Gaddin

A must-read book for all Christians who may have difficulty with reconciling evangelical teaching in regard to sexuality and their own intuition and instincts. The author artfully synchronizes scripture, church history, cultural diversity, Hebrew and Greek word meanings and human instinct, enabling a Christian man or woman to safely question their beliefs regarding sexuality. The author also accurately articulates the rightful role of women in society, in the family, and in the church, which may come as a surprise to many evangelicals. A highly interesting and informational book.

—Penelope Middleton

Liberation is spoken of 45 times in the New Testament. But it's missed because it is translated "salvation" to change the focus to the after life instead of life on earth.

—PropheticImagination
@PropheticCenter

# PREFACE

I sat in church today, frustrated and irritated again as the pastor preached from Matthew 5:28 on Jesus's statement about lusting after a woman. How is it that educated individuals with doctorate degrees can't come to terms with the understanding of what lust is and what lust isn't according to the Bible?

On my way home, I voiced my frustration to my wife regarding the old-school line about lust and this being every man's battle and how he must resist the temptation. Finally, my wife said, "I really think you should go ahead and write the book on biblical sexuality that you have been meaning to do for so long."

So with this encouragement from my wife, and yet with trepidation, I launch into the unknown waters. The purpose of this book is an endeavor to set men and women free from guilt and bondage. This would be a noble purpose. Correct? And yet I am acutely aware that while an animal is caged and fed and cared for properly, it is also relatively safe. If I let the animal out, it will be free; but will it be safe?

Will it use its freedom to hurt others and ultimately destroy itself?

This is the reason for my reluctance. And yet the thought comes to me that I have no right to keep a person in guilt or bondage when I have the key to set them free, and I am not responsible for what the released prisoner will do with their freedom.

My prayer is that you, the reader, will find new freedom, and you will surrender that freedom to the leadership and lordship of the Holy Spirit and that you will live your life according to the example of love and righteousness as modeled by Christ himself.

# INTRODUCTION

I am a hopeless romantic. Genuine, real-life love stories always pull at my heartstrings. I read a story about fifty years ago, when I was in my early twenties, that I will never forget. It was a story about a young man from California in the gold rush days. After the California gold rush subsided, the next big find was in Alaska. And so this young man joined the thousands of those heading to find gold in the far North. He went to an area where there was a little town. Up in the mountains, above the town, he put down his roots. He was highly successful as a gold prospector and eventually started a building enterprise that was one of the most profitable businesses in the area.

It so happened that in the course of time, with his occasional need to go into the small town for supplies, he met and began a relationship with a beautiful young woman from England. She was the daughter of one of the town's store owners, and they fell madly in love. After some time, the young Californian decided he needed to either marry her or terminate the relationship so she would be able to find a suitable husband. So one evening, he took her back into the mountains and on to a lookout where they had a spectacular view of the valley below. He told her that he loved her more than she could ever imagine; but unfortunately, he could not marry her, and because he loved her so much, he had to terminate the relationship so that she would be able to find a suitable husband.

She was of course heartbroken and asked him repeatedly why he could not marry her. She asked him if he was already married, and he said that he wasn't. He held her in his arms the entire night as she wept and slept intermittently. In the morning, he took her back to town, and they parted forever. He returned to his business in the mountains, and it was only a matter of time before he got word that she had become engaged to another man. He immediately sent a construction crew to the town to build a church for her and her fiancé to get married in.

The whole area was aware of what was happening, but no one knew why he could not marry her except an old woman who had known him in California. Many people tried to get the secret out of her but to no avail. Eventually, she came close to dying and decided to tell a close friend who, upon the lady's death, decided to reveal the secret. The young man had been a Catholic priest in California and had therefore taken the vow of celibacy. He had rejected the priesthood but believed that there was no way out for him from the vow of celibacy.

It is a story that brings pain to my heart even as I write this fifty years later. To think that two young people who had so much love for each other could not find the fulfillment of that love because of the false teaching of the Christian church regarding sexuality. Over the years, I have often imaged what I would have said to that young man if I had been a Christian minister in that little town and had been aware of his predicament.

This book is therefore dedicated to the memory of the young couple from California and England who were destined to meet in Alaska and who remain nameless, along with the millions of others who have experienced the loss of the love of their lives due to the church's cruel and erroneous biblical teaching on sexuality. If you are one of those millions, it is my deep prayer and hope that you will find the healing of your heart and life through God's incredible grace.

CHAPTER 1

# BIBLICAL MYTH BUSTERS

The first myth that needs to be debunked regarding biblical sexuality is that sex outside of marriage is wrong and sinful. It is an absurdity to look at the complex world of marriage, both from a cultural perspective and a historical perspective, to arrive at such a wild conclusion.

Before we look at this incorrect teaching prevalent in the evangelical and fundamental churches of today, we must first find some definition of marriage. From a biblical perspective, there is none. We have no record that Adam and Eve were married. Rather, we read that God made Eve and gave her to Adam.

"For this reason, a man will leave his father and mother and be united to his wife and will become one flesh"—i.e., have sex (Genesis 2:24).

But what does the word "wife" mean? This is the first time it appears in biblical history. Of course, we immediately assume that the word "wife" means all the things that we associate with that word in our Western culture. But to do so is to make a grave mistake. If we take the biblical text pure and simple as it is written, it simply means the woman that a man has sex with (i.e., one flesh). There is not one single suggestion of anything further than this. Paul even made reference to this in talking about prostitution when he said that a man that has sex with a prostitute has married her (1 Corinthians 6:15).

As strange as it may seem, there is no other biblical definition of marriage. Not only is there no definition given of marriage, but more to the point, there is absolutely no statement or reference in the Bible that sex is for marriage only, even if we did have a clear definition of it.

Marriage, or the idea of marriage, has developed over the ages through thousands of years, cultures, and religions to be something incredibly different, depending on both the time period and/or the culture.

Firstly, let's look at the Old Testament concept of marriage. Because the male was physically stronger than the female, it didn't take men long to set up a male-dominated society and to make rules and customs that benefited men and not women. For example, in the Old Testament, women (including wives and daughters) had no better status than animals. Men owned them and had the power of life and death over them. Conversely, women could own nothing and had no power over their lives at all.

This was the reason that we read of the women of the Bible being so concerned that they had a son. The reason was that if something happened to their husbands, they had no recourse other than prostitution or begging. A loving husband could not leave anything to his wife or daughters even if he wanted to. They would be destitute. When a man died, in biblical times, it was customary that all his possessions would be inherited by his sons. However, what happened if the man had no sons? If this was the case, the elders of the village would come to his home and seek to find a legitimate heir. The questions they would ask would be, "Did he have any other wives?" "Did he have any concubines (live-in girlfriends)?" They would go to the village brothels and ask the prostitutes if any of them had had any sons from him. They would visit the slave girls to see if he had any sons among the slave girls. If they found a son, then they would decree that all of the deceased man's possessions be given to this new-found son, including his wives, concubines, and daughters.

What if they could find no son? In this case, all of his possessions would be given to the most senior male slave, including all the women in his family. If he had no male slaves, all of his possessions, including all the women, would be divided up between his closest male relatives. The new owners could do with the women whatever they wanted to, including selling them into slavery, putting them out on the street for prostitution, or killing them.

Can you see why the women of the Bible were apparently so concerned about having a son? We must also bear in mind that, in the Old Testament, not only could men have as many wives as they wanted, or concubines, but they were free to have sex with any other woman unless she was married to someone else.

Growing up in the church and becoming aware of the stories of the Bible, I was always confused with the story of the woman taken in adultery as recorded in Mathew 5:27. I thought it took two to tango. It was only years later that I found out that, in biblical times, it was perfectly acceptable for a man to have sex outside of marriage, and it was the woman who had to be put to death because she should not have tempted him.

So let's get this straight. The church today maintains that sex should be reserved only for marriage. But even in the New Testament, which is the basis of our Christian teaching, it was okay for a married man to have sex with another woman because she tempted him. Doesn't that make a mockery of the position held by a large section of the church today?

When we start to analyze all the stories of the Bible involving sex, we find that the evangelical and fundamentalist's view of sex is not simply on dangerous ground, but rather, they have no ground at all on which to stand.

*Biblical evidence A*

Probably the most convincing story in the Bible regarding this subject involves King David. I suppose, most people would agree that if there was a single time in their lives whereby they would want to be in perfect harmony with God's laws and precepts, it would be just before they died.

With King David in (1 Kings 2:2), we find that because he was dying, the leaders of the nation, which would include the high priest and spiritual leaders, went out and found a young girl named Abishag for him to have sex with in the hopes that it would give him the will to live and revive him.

Now as it happened, he didn't have sex with her because, as yet, Viagra hadn't been invented. Some could justifiably argue that he didn't have sex because he wasn't married to her, except for the fact that he also had concubines that he had sex with but wasn't married to. Some may argue that the leaders got Abishag to simply be his nurse and lie next to him and keep him warm. If that was the case, why does the record state that the leaders looked for a beautiful virgin to do this? Beautiful virgins in a patriarchal society are only sought out for one thing—sex. Let's not be naive. She was brought to him for sexual purposes.

Regardless of the reason as to why David didn't have sex with Abishag, we can't escape the fact that he was not the instigator of the event. The people who brought Abishag to him were the spiritual and national leaders. It was therefore obvious that, in their minds, there was absolutely nothing wrong with David, the "man after God's own heart" (1 Samuel 13:14), having sex with a girl he was not married to right before he had to stand before his Maker.

There is also an additional interesting twist to this story. After David died and Solomon became king, his older brother, Adonijah, approached Bathsheba (Solomon's mother) to ask if he could have Abishag for his wife. Bethsheba went with the request to her son Solomon. He went ballistic and had Adonijah executed.

What's the significance of this? It shows very clearly that Abishag was not simply a nurse or attendant but now had the status of a royal wife, even though David never married her, and Adonijah's request for her to be his wife was a direct threat to Solomon's hold on the throne.

*Biblical evidence B*

In Genesis chapter 16, we have the story of Abraham and Hagar. Sarah was tired of waiting for a son and told Abraham to go and have sex with her slave girl, Hagar. Because Abraham owned Hagar, any children that she gave birth to would belong to him. I guess Sarah was betting on being able to raise any son that Hagar had as her own, which would give her the material security that she craved.

By rights, she could have had Abraham sell Hagar and keep any children of Hagar as her own, who in turn would care for her if Abraham died. So Abraham, as a dutiful husband, went and had sex with Hagar who produced a son, which he called Ishmael.

Up until this point, all is going to plan. Hagar had a boy, which in essence would become Sarah's son and security. However, what Sarah didn't bargain for was that Abraham would become emotionally attached to his son and therefore start giving preference to his mother, Hagar.

She was not just Sarah's slave girl anymore but the mother of his son. The whole family dynamic had changed. Of course, this was compounded by the fact that now Hagar developed a superior attitude over Sarah because she had the crown jewel—a son

Sarah saw the writing on the wall and realized that Ishmael's allegiance would always be to his mother over her, no matter how much she schemed and planned. She also realized that when Abraham died, Ishmael would receive everything that Abraham owned and that she would be thrown under the bus. She complained to Abraham about the situation. He, being a typical man, didn't want to be bothered by women's little quarrels and issues and, being the man of the house that he was, told Sarah she could do whatever she wanted to do.

Consequently, Sarah turned both Hagar and little Ishmael out into the desert and told them to get lost. It's strange how God didn't forsake Hagar and Ishmael. Instead, He promised her that Ishmael would become the father of many nations and, as we know, is father of all the Arabs.

One would think that if Abraham or Hagar had done something wrong by having sex outside of marriage that God would have punished them or at least ignored or abandoned them. No. Instead, He blessed them. What a strange God we have who blesses and cares for people who have sex outside of marriage.

Now here is the interesting thing. Abraham has been rightly called *the* father of the faithful. He was called this because he believed God when God said that "he would be the father of many nations and was justified because of this faith"(Genesis 15:6). Once again, we have absolutely no reference or suggestion in the whole Bible of Abraham doing anything wrong or sinful in having sex with Hagar.

*Biblical evidence C*

The ancient biblical world had another backup plan also, which later became part of the Mosaic law and commanded by God.

It was ordered by God that the brother of a deceased man must have sex with his brother's widow and give her children. But then there is a slight twist. Any sons born from this arrangement would be entered into the chronological history as sons of the dead brother and not of the biological brother. Furthermore, all the dead brother's inheritance would go to the sons fathered by the living brother.

Now we have an account of such a thing happening in Genesis chapter 38, but an interesting thing happened. Judah, who was one of the most righteous of all of Jacob's sons, had three sons: Er, Onan, and Kezib. Er did something wrong, and God killed him. The Bible says that Jacob commanded his second son, Onan, to go and have sex with his dead brother's widow (no mention of him marrying her). His words to Onan were, "Do your duty to produce offspring for your brother" (Genesis 38:8). Onan went and had sex with her, as was ordered by God. But before he ejaculated, he pulled himself out, and his semen fell on the ground. It was obvious therefore that he did not want his sister-in-law to become pregnant. What happened? Wait for the drumroll. God struck him dead because he wouldn't have proper sex with his sister-in-law who he was NOT married to.

There is a powerful teaching in this story and from future Mosaic law, which is that God is far more concerned about men caring for the widows and orphans than he is about who they have sex with.

*Biblical evidence D*

The story of the twelve sons of Jacob is very interesting in relation to the topic of biblical sexuality. Jacob had two wives, Rachel and her sister Leah. Each had a servant. Rachael's servant was Bilhah, and Leah's servant was Zilpah. Rachael's sons were Joseph and Benjamin, and Leah's sons were Reuben, Simeon, Levi, Judah, Issachar, and Zebulon.

Now we read in Genesis chapter 30 that both Rachael and Leah, at different times and for some reason, each gave their servant girls to Jacob, "as a wife." He therefore had sex with them both. Rachael's servant, Bilhah, gave birth to Dan and Naphtali, and Leah's servant, Zilpah, gave birth to Gad and Asher.

Now it is interesting to note that, in both instances, we have this expression, "gave as a wife," and the only thing that changed in the domestic situation was that Jacob started having sex with them.

By definition, as already stated, Jacob was now married to all four women.

Doesn't it therefore seem preposterous that, in today's world, there are sections of the church that would try to say that any couple living together and having sex outside of our definition of marriage are "living in sin" when, in fact, this is the only definition of biblical marriage that we have?

But there is also a further point of interest in this story. For nowhere, absolutely nowhere, in the Bible is there any reference to any distinction between any of the sons, or tribes, based on who their mother was. In fact, it would be safe to say that even the average pastor, minister, or biblical scholar could not tell you which mother gave birth to which son other than Rachael being the mother of Joseph and Benjamin.

Some might know that Leah was the mother of Levi and Judah because they became significant tribes in Israel. This is because the Bible makes no distinction between the sons of the two legitimate married wives or the sons of slave girls. And why doesn't the Bible make any distinction? Because, biblically, there isn't any distinction.

*Biblical evidence E*

In Exodus chapter 22, God gave the law, which in part again relates to sexuality. In verses 16 through 17, we read, "If a man seduces a virgin, who is pledged to be married, and sleeps with her he must pay the bride price and she shall be his wife. If the father absolutely refuses to give her to him, he must still pay the bride price for virgins."

Now this is an interesting statement. It is clear that the issue here is not sexual immorality by a man and woman having sex outside of marriage but simply one of economics from the father's point of view. A daughter's value was only in her economic value in obtaining a good bride price for her as a virgin. But if a man seduced her and had sex with her, the father loses a large amount of money. The man must therefore pay the bride price even if the father doesn't want to give her to the man in marriage.

For, virtually, every command that God gives in the Bible, there is a consequence for violation. If it was wrong or sinful for the man to have sex with a girl because they were not married, God would have followed through with what the punishment was.

However, there is not even any suggestion of moral or sexual wrong doing apart from the financial implications to the father.

*Biblical evidence F*

In Leviticus chapter 18, we have a list of people that a man can't have sex with. It is basically a law against incest and bestiality and lists the following: mother, father's other wives, stepmother, sister, half sister, daughter-in-law, granddaughter, aunt, sister-in-law, both woman and her daughter together, neighbors' wife, other men, animals.

If it was sinful to have sex with anyone outside of marriage, God would have put it in this list. This is the list of sexual taboos, including homosexuality and bestiality, and yet God said absolutely nothing about having sex outside of marriage, nor did he say a man should only have one wife.

If I was a car salesman and you came to look for a car to buy, what would you think if I made the following statement: "None of the blue, gray, or white cars are for sale"? You would take from that statement that ALL the other cars ARE for sale.

By God specifically telling us who we couldn't have sex with, He was, by inference, telling us who we could have sex with, which is obviously those that aren't on that list.

Probably, at this stage, the reader is aware that I have only drawn from the Old Testament for examples of sexual behavior. I can hear someone saying, "What about all the references in the New Testament regarding fornication?"

Good question. But what is fornication? For years, the evangelical and Fundamentalist Churches have said that adultery was having sex with a married person who wasn't your spouse and that fornication was two people having sex who were not married to anyone, including each other. With regard to adultery, their definition is correct.

**With regard to fornication the church simply lied to us. Fornication is not sexual relations between two unmarried people.**

The word fornication comes from the Latin word *fornix*, meaning "arch," and was used as a euphemism for "brothel." The first recorded use in English is in the Cursor Mundi, c. 1300. The *Oxford English Dictionary* records a figurative use as well: "the forsaking of God for idols."

"Fornicated," as an adjective, is still used in botany, meaning "arched" or "bending over" (as in a leaf). Hence the expression "fern and fauna," plants which arch. In architecture, the term refers to a vault. It will come as a surprise therefore to realize that all the great cathedrals of the world are both pornographic and fornicated in their architecture. So with the joint meaning of a vaulted arch, what do we come up with? The Colosseum in Rome was built upon vaulted arches. And under these arches, at night, was where all types of sexual perversion took place.

In 1 Corinthians, incest, homosexual intercourse, and prostitution are all explicitly forbidden by name. Paul was preaching about activities based on Levitical sexual prohibitions. It is these, and only these, behaviors that are intended by Paul's prohibition in chapter 7.

Charles Troy made the following statement:

> Another example of premarital sex in the Old Testament is given in Deuteronomy 21:10. This is the case in which a man takes a woman captive, and then, if he wants to make her his wife, he must follow the conditions it sets forth and then have intercourse with her. Then if she is found to be desirable, he has the option of marrying her or sending her away. This passage not only condones premarital sex but maybe even divorce as well.

I cannot think of any other passage of scripture that so clearly debunks the concept that sex outside of marriage is wrong as this one does.

From "The Week" we have the following regarding; The Origins of Marriage:

"The best available evidence suggests that it's about 4,350 years old. For thousands of years before that, most anthropologists believe, families consisted of loosely organized groups of as many as 30 people, with several male leaders, multiple women shared by them, and children. As hunter-gatherers settled down into agrarian civilizations, society had a need for more stable arrangements. The first recorded evidence of marriage ceremonies uniting one woman and one man dates from about 2350 BC in Mesopotamia. Over the next several hundred years, marriage evolved into a widespread institution embraced by the ancient Hebrews, Greeks, and Romans. But back then, marriage had little to do with love or with religion. **What was it about then?**

"Marriage's primary purpose was to bind women to men and thus guarantee that a man's children were truly his biological heirs. Through marriage, a woman became a man's property. In the betrothal ceremony of ancient Greece, a father would hand over his daughter with these words: I pledge my daughter for the purpose of producing legitimate offspring. Among the ancient Hebrews, men were free to take several wives. Married Greeks and Romans were free to satisfy their sexual urges with concubines, prostitutes, and even teenage male lovers, while their wives were required to stay home and tend to the household. If wives failed to produce offspring, their husbands could give them back and marry someone else.

"For much of human history, couples were brought together for practical reasons, not because they fell in love. In time, of course, many marriage partners came to feel deep mutual love and devotion. But the idea of romantic love, as a motivating force for marriage, only goes as far back as the Middle Ages.

When colonists first came to America, at a time when polygamy was still accepted in most parts of the world, the husband's dominance was officially recognized under a legal doctrine called coverture, under which the new bride's identity was absorbed into his. The bride gave up her name to symbolize the surrendering of her identity, and the husband suddenly became more important, as the official public representative of two people, not one. The rules were so strict that any American woman who married a foreigner immediately lost her citizenship.

"The idea that marriage is a private relationship for the fulfillment of two individuals is really very new, said historian Stephanie Coontz, author of *The Way We Never Were: American Families and the Nostalgia Trap.* Within the past forty years, marriage has changed more than in the last five thousand years."

Ahlgrim said, "Although lots of people are married in the Bible, there are no descriptions of any ceremonies. Adam and Eve were 'married' simply by the fact that they were made for each other and they procreate. Jacob married Leah by mistake, which happened not because of a disguised bride at a wedding ceremony but because he consummated the marriage in the darkness of a tent. Jesus attended a wedding in Cana, which consisted of a family party, but no ceremony is described. The reason there are no marriage ceremonies in the Bible is because marriage did not involve a ceremony.

**Marriage, in the Bible, simply consists of a man and woman, with the consent of the woman's father or guardian, living together and attempting procreation.**

No vows, no priest, no ritual, no prayer, no pronouncement, no license, no registration. This is quite different from how we define and enact marriage today. For many Christians, a marriage is not a Christian marriage unless it is officiated by a credentialed minister who makes a verbal pronouncement, preferably in the presence of the congregation.

But these are all recent innovations. For most of human history, marriage has simply been an agreement, recognized or arranged by their immediate families, for a man and woman to live together.

**Marriage, as a legal institution and as a religious ceremony, began as a result of the reformation.**

Beginning in the Middle Ages, churches kept records of who was married to whom. But Luther viewed marriage as a "worldly matter," and so he turned over the recording of marriages to the state.

The Catholic Church did not require marriages to be officiated by a priest until 1563, and the Anglican Church did not get around to making this requirement until 1753. So for the past five hundred years, there have been, in the European tradition, three kinds of marriage: legal, religious, and social. But social marriage, strictly speaking, is the most biblical.

## What would happen if the church today were to once again recognize social marriage?

It would mean that couples living together, particularly those raising children, could be treated as married even if they are not legally married or have not undergone any kind of religious ritual. Indeed, during most of history, society, as well as the church, would have regarded such couples as married.

Since a growing number of couples today are choosing to live together and raise children without a ceremony or legal license, it may be advantageous for the church to look more kindly and inclusively upon them. Otherwise, we will alienate these couples, and they will not benefit from the guidance and support of the church. This does not mean the church should stop advocating for religious ceremonies and legalized marriages. These innovations have important purposes. A public ceremony that includes vows and prayers makes the couple's commitment to each other clear, links the couple's love to the sacred story of God's love, and gives the community and congregation an explicitly supportive role in helping to maintain the marriage. A legally recognized marriage gives the couple various rights and benefits, provides additional stability to the relationship, and protects both spouses and children in case of divorce. The church supports marriage and family the best, I think, when it recognizes that couples who intend to share their lives together represent a type of marriage.

Hannah of "Rosewood and Olive" wrote,

> The biblical meaning of what it means to be married and what constitutes 'morally acceptable sex' is actually a highly debated topic. There are some pastors who, though they *do* believe it is a sin to live together, still believe it is better to marry the couple so they will *not* continue to live in sin. However, there are also pastors and Bible scholars who do *not* believe it is a sin to live together because they do not hold the belief that marriage begins after a ceremony is performed or once you obtain your marriage license—since marriages in the Bible did not require the government's permission to be 'officially' married. Instead, some believe that marriage begins when a man and a woman have made a commitment in their hearts to each other before God and have consummated the marriage by becoming "one flesh." There are other biblical scholars who believe the Greek word *porneia* has been translated incorrectly altogether—which is where the English translation of 'sexual immorality' comes from.

J. T. Anderson said,

> First off, "premarital sex" is a misnomer. It's an invention of the Catholic church. The Scriptures make it very easy to determine who you can and can't have sex with and when you can and can't have sex. So we're really dealing with

a leftover question from Catholic doctrine that Protestants never resolved. The great sleight of hand the Catholic church pulled on believers was requiring a license (i.e., permission) in order to marry a woman or engage in sexual intercourse. In the Scriptures, you will find absolutely ZERO requirements (or even examples) of a man getting permission from the government or a priest to have sex with or marry a woman.

CHAPTER **2**

# CULTURAL DEFINITIONS OF MARRIAGE

The second issue we need to consider is with regard to what kind of marriage we are talking about when we say that sex outside of marriage is wrong. We make an incorrect assumption that the marriage that is part of our Western, Judeo-Christian culture is universal.

**Marriage, and what constitutes marriage, is as varied and as diverse as the cultures, countries, and religions of the world.**

So let's look at some of them.

The Australian Aborigines are a very nomadic people and live a simple lifestyle. Their tribal clans are usually matriarchal, meaning that they have a head woman who has the final say or at least an influential say in what happens in the community.

When boy likes girl, he tries to be with her, and her brothers chase him away. If she is interested in him, she will make a small pathway to her house with white stones on either side of the path. This tells the boy that she is interested. He continues to try to see her, and her brothers continue to chase him away. Finally, the matri-

16

archal woman in the village tells the brothers to leave him alone. This means they are now married.

So let's digest this. If Grandma says she's cool with Mary and Bill having sex, then according to their culture, are they married?

Now let's slip over to India where there are hundreds of different tribes, clans, and subclans. In some areas of India, if a woman and a man are simply seen to be eating together, they are considered to be married.

In other clans, the woman doesn't even have to eat with a man but simply prepare him a meal, and they are considered married.

How many men have taken a woman out to dinner? Dumb question. We all have. So according to a clan in India, you became married to that woman.

Now let's fly over to Kenya and visit the wonderful Maasai people on the edge of the great Serengeti. When a young boy goes through initiation in early teens, he becomes a man and a hunter and warrior. All the boys that go through the same initiation ceremony with him stay as a bonded group right through their lives—something resembling a closely bonded graduation class. When they reach thirty years of age, they have a large marriage ceremony, and all of them are married and now they are no longer hunters and warriors but elders. However, every man in that group has sexual accesses to every wife within the group. They share and share alike.

Now let's go to Tibet. The custom in Tibet is for several men (usually brothers) to share one wife. She is the wife of all of them.

Let's duck over to the Middle East. In most Muslim countries, prostitution is forbidden. However, prostitution often thrives when it is forbidden by both the religion and the state. How can this be?

When a man wants to have sex with a prostitute, he goes down to the local brothel and picks out the woman he wants for the night. They then both go to the front desk and sign the necessary documents and get married. When they come downstairs the next morning for breakfast, the divorce papers are all ready for them to sign at the front desk. They go their separate ways, and everybody is happy (in a manner of speaking)

In Thailand, when a young girl reaches marriageable age, she asks her father to build her a little hut, like a tree house, in the back yard. She then moves into the tree house and puts the word out that she is looking for a husband. The interested young men come and see her in her tree house. If she wants to, they spend the night or as many nights as she chooses having sex with each one of them so she can make the best choice as to the one she wants to marry.

There are some areas of the primitive world where a couple is not allowed to get married until they have produced a child together.

In South America, there are tribes who stipulate that all the men in the village must have sex with the potential bride before she can be married. It usually takes several weeks. Let me ask a valid question, "If you were a missionary working with these people, would you advocate that women get married or refrain from marriage?" Yes. See, these issues do not fit our paradigms of black and white, right or wrong, do they? And God certainly doesn't have the same paradigms that we have.

Finally, the most powerful piece of biblical evidence that we have is that of ancient Egypt where there was really no such thing as marriage. The closest thing they had was that if a man and a woman lived with each other, they were considered married. There was absolutely nothing else they needed to do but move in with each other.

There has always been a question as to whether Cleopatra was the wife of Mark Antony or his mistress. The answer is, she was both, for there was no distinction between the two in ancient Egypt. However, this brings something very interesting into the equation. This means that Joseph was never married according to any standard of marriage that we could propose. The woman he took as his wife was simply his mistress; and by being his mistress, she was his wife. So now we have one of the most righteous men who ever lived, and one of the few who had not one single blemish on his godly character, spending the whole of his adult life "living in sin," if our modern perverted theology was in fact the truth.

However, the plot thickens. Joseph was also a man who held himself to an incredibly strict code of sexual conduct. As you will remember, his boss's wife wanted to have sex with him, and Joseph refused, saying, "It would be a sin against God" and called it evil (Genesis 39:9), obviously because he knew it would be adultery. She continued to endeavor to seduce him to the point of pulling of his clothes (verse 12). But he ran from the house and spent seven years in prison because Potiphar's wife lied to her husband, saying that Joseph had tried to rape her (verses 13–20) Yes, I know "hell hath no fury like a woman scorned." So I repeat, here we have a man of impeccable, godly character, especial when it came to sexual conduct, and yet he lived his life with a woman he was not married to in any form of marriage that we would consider today.

So when the church makes statements saying that "it is wrong for Christians to have sex outside of marriage," it begs the question, "What marriage are we talking about?"

Of course, the answer would probably be, "A Christian marriage."

Before we look to the Bible for clues as to what a Christian marriage would look like, let's first look at what a biblical marriage was in the Old Testament.

According to the Old Testament, marriage means a man can have as many wives and concubines as he chooses and can have sex with any woman as long as she is not someone else's wife. It also means he has the power of life and death over her and her children, to do with as he wishes. The man can divorce his wife any time he chooses and throw her out in the street where her only recourse would be prostitution or begging, but a woman could never divorce her husband no matter how terrible the circumstances.

Now let's move to the New Testament. As incredible as it may seem, there is no change in what constitutes marriage in the NT from the OT except for the following: Husbands are to love their wives as Christ loved the church (a radical concept for that day and age and would negate the power of life or death he had over his wife). Wives must obey their husbands. Actually, that's not what Paul said at all. The Greek word he used for "obey" was the same as that of the order for a Roman soldier's armor-bearer to stand by and hold his armor while he fights. Literal interpretation? "Stand together to face the world."

So to summarize, according to the Bible, this is what a Christian marriage would look like:

1. A man and woman living together
2. The husband may have any number of other wives and concubines.
3. The husband can have sex with any other woman who is not married. But if a woman does that, she is stoned to death.
4. A man can divorce his wife any time he wants to, but a woman could never divorce her husband.
5. Husbands must love their wives as Christ loved the church.
6. Wives must stand with their husbands.

There we have the sum total of what the Bible has to say about marriage. Are you still sure you want a Christian marriage?

Very little of what we do in a wedding ceremony and very little of our modern concept of a Christian marriage has any biblical basis at all. Let's look at some of the things that have developed over the ages without any biblical foundation.

1. Choosing our married partner
2. Marrying for love
3. A commitment made for life
4. Monogamous
5. Keeping sex only for marriage.
6. "To have and to hold, for richer and for poorer, in sickness and in health"
7. Forsaking all others
8. Wedding ring
9. Getting married in a church
10. Having a clergyman perform a ceremony and making a pronouncement of marriage
11. Marriage licenses
12. Marriage certificate

All of these things have developed down through the ages by both the church and the state and may have noble and honorable objectives, but none of them have any scriptural mandate.

The concept of a wedding was not present for thousands of years. The word "wedding" comes from the word "wed," which literal means "to pay the bride price."

So basically, in bygone times, all that happened was that the groom paid the father the money, and that was the "wed." Hence they were married. Or simply put, buying a wife was the definition of marriage.

Historically, this is where the role of the best man came in. The role of the best man was to guard the bride while the groom paid the father the bride price. The woman had spent her whole life being protected by her father; and once she was married, she would be protected by her husband. But for a short time, she was very vulnerable as the father and groom completed their business transaction. So the best man was the bride's personal body guard until all the business was taken care of.

Have you ever noticed how a groom always has his best friend be the best man? That was because, in ancient times, his best friend was the only man he could trust to either not violate his bride or kidnap her.

The question is, "How did marriage develop down through the ages to what we have today?"

This is by no means meant to be an exhaustive or conclusive account of the history of marriage. However, we can look at some basic reasons as to how marriage became what it is today.

A.    Practical

The first reason the concept of marriage developed was for purely practical reasons. A woman needed someone to protect her, provide for her, and to give her children. A man, on the other hand, needed someone to cook meals, care for the home and the children, and be able to have sex on a regular basis without going to a lot of effort to find it or costing him anything.

In essence, it would have been almost impossible for either a man or a woman to survive, let alone prosper in primitive cultures without this kind of arrangement.

I can site the example of my own grandfather. His father was a pioneer and settler of a colony in the far-flung corners of the British Empire in the late 1800s, and he ran a sheep farm. He lived in a remote rural area of the country far from any help. He came in from the fields one day to find his wife dead on the floor and his child, about one year old who was my grandfather, crying and banging his dead mother's body with an empty milk bottle because he was hungry.

My grandfather also had an older brother who was about three or four years of age. So here was the dilemma. How does a man run a farm in a desolate and lonely rural area of a remote European colony and at the same time take care for his toddler and baby all by himself? The answer is, he couldn't. So he had to do the only thing he could do to survive and immediately married a widow from a neighboring farm. She turned out to be the proverbial wicked stepmother, but that's another story.

For hundreds of years, in Europe, if a father could not find a husband for his daughter, he would consign her to a nunnery for life as a nun. Conversely, a young man could not marry until he had enough money to care for his wife. So marriage was primarily based on the practical principle that both men and women mutually needed each other. Love had nothing to do with it.

B.   Economic

The second reason was economic. Sons were always a welcome addition to a family because, when they grew up, they could enhance the family business, or farm, and would do so until their father died. He could end up a wealthy man if he had many sons. Besides, the sons would eventually marry, and they would have their own sons who would work on the farm also. All that free manpower also provided the old guy with his own little private militia. This was not only great for protection but could also be used to intimidate a rival into accepting favorable terms with business transactions. It was capitalism at its finest.

But where is the financial advantage in having a daughter? Not only does she require the cost of feeding and raising, but just about the time she reaches her teenage years and could be of some help on the farm, she would want to marry and run off and work for her new husband's father. What a bad investment daughters were. However, they did have some redeemable financial value. If the father could marry them off and get a good bride price as soon as possible, then he might not only get his money back but make a little on the side. However, there was a large condition to be kept if he was going to get the best price for her. She had to be a virgin. If she wasn't a virgin, it would almost be impossible to sell her.

Are you starting to see where the custom of the necessity of being a virgin at the time of marriage started and what motivated it and propagated the myth even to this day?

C.   To protect the lineage

Most historians agree that one of the most influential events in human history was when we changed from being hunters and gatherers to gardeners and growers. This massive sea change now created a new problem to be addressed, which was the need to own land and establish property rights. Being hunters and gatherers, ancient peoples simply roamed a free landscape, taking all their animals and tents with them. They were totally nomadic. However, with the new phenomenon of growing crops, the need arose to stay in one place and put down roots and the establishment of property ownership. However, with this new social order came the problem of what happens to the land when the patriarchal leader dies. So it was established that the family could stay and claim ownership as long as the new owner was a male protégé of the patriarchal father. This is where the whole issue of linage arose. How does one prove that one's son is his and that his women had not become pregnant by another man?

This becomes the primary reason that a virgin was worth more than a nonvirgin. No, it wasn't for more sexual enjoyment, although no doubt it was a factor, however probably a very small factor due to the fact that a man could have sex with any woman that he owned. A far greater factor, however, was that by buying a virgin, a man had insurance that he would be the father of her child.

If he married a nonvirgin, there was no way he would ever know for sure that any child born after nine months of marriage would be his. It was conceivable (no pun intended) that she could be already pregnant, and there would be no way to prove who the father was. Now that had dangerous implications.

Let's say Sue is pregnant to Steve when she marries Bill. When little Johnny is born, the issue is just not one of who is the father but, more importantly, if Bill is not the father of Johnny, who is?

Let's fast-forward the video a few decades. Things may not be going well in the family. Sue tells Johnny that Bill is not his father, but that Steve is. On that basis, everything that Johnny has inherited, according to law, becomes Steve's as he is the father of Johnny. (Woe is me, shame and scandal in the family.) War breaks out between father and supposed son; and everything that Bill has worked for his entire life goes up in smoke, including his life.

Was there any kind of insurance against this type of thing happening? Yes, just one—virginity. This was the reason why, in ancient times, virginity became such a valuable commodity. By marrying a virgin, a man not only had a watertight insurance policy, he also owned the insurance company.

A Greek orator in the fourth century BC explained it this way: "One of the most important functions of marriage was the production of legitimate children who would honor the father in his old age, show respect to the ancestors and clan gods, and perpetuate the family property. We have the courtesans for pleasure, concubines for the daily care of our bodies, but wives to bear us legitimate children and to be the trust guardians of our household."

Under Athenian law, a man's seduction of another man's wife was punishable by death, but the rape of another man's wife merited only a fine. Why the drastic distinction? Because the first would be done secretly and could bring an illegitimate child into the family without the husband knowing; but with the rapist, at least he knew that if his wife became pregnant, she only had to wait nine months and then get rid of the baby or at least keep it for a slave. But at least the husband would know that it was not his child, so no big deal.

## Polluting the family linage was the greatest crime of all.

The historian Bulwer made the following statement: "The Greeks had little pleasure in the society of their wives. At first, a young husband only visited her by stealth: to be seen in company with her was a disgrace."

The clearest example of protecting the purity of the linage is found in the lives of Britain's royal family. Throughout the Middle Ages, the king and queen could not have sex unless it was witnessed by the leaders of the nation, including leaders of the church. They lived at each end of the royal castles. The king could have sex with whoever he wanted. In fact, the British parliament would publicly announce, and put in the press, the amount of allocated stipend they were giving to the king's mistress. But the queen was restricted.

The reason for this was so that they would all know with a certainty that any baby she produced would in fact be from the king and therefore the legitimate heir to the throne.

As time went on, they realized that this was not the most becoming way to ensure the purity of the kingly line and therefore changed to mandating that all future queens should be a virgin when she married. So a doctor would certify that she was a virgin, or the marriage would not take place.

This practice became part of the culture, resulting in our accepted belief that all women who were not previously married must be virgins. Because whatever the royal family did, the population did in an endeavor to emulate them.

So what's all this got to do with sexuality today? It portrays the picture of all men in biblical times who were paranoid about their wives having sex with another man and therefore resulting in the child inheriting his name and fortune. This was the primary motivation for the punishment of stoning for married women who had sex with any man other than her husband and the paramount importance of marrying only a virgin.

It is from these two practical needs of the times that the importance of a virgin marriage arose and had little, if anything, to do with sinfulness or purity. There may be some cynicism of the fact that the practice of virgin marriages by British royalty was the basis of forming a culture in the Christian Western world that has extended to this day. Don't be deceived, an incredible amount of the culture and customs of the modern Western world came from England. Do you know why men wear pants with a sharp crease in the front and back?

When Prince Edward was out hunting one day, at the turn of the last century, he was caught out in a torrential downpour of rain. He took refuge in a farmer's cottage, and the farmer and his wife gave him their bed for the night. In an effort to dry out his wet pants, the farmer's wife put them under her made-up bed on the floor and hoped that the warmth of her body would dry them out by morning. It did, but they also had a distinct crease down the back and front of his pants. When he arrived in London the next day, all the crowds and newspapers saw the king's new "fashion statement," and that is why you still have creases in your pants today.

It wasn't just kings and queens who didn't sleep with each other except to have sex. It has been the practice for most cultures for centuries. So when did it become fashionable for husbands and wives to sleep with each other on a regular basis as they do today?

Unfortunately, we have to go back to England. When Queen Victoria married Prince Albert of Germany, she ordered by royal decree that he would sleep in her bed every night—smart woman. And so she started another fashion of husbands and wives sleeping in the same bed every night.

Queen Victoria also started the fashion of brides wearing white. It had nothing to do with some symbol of purity. The reason was simple: She wanted to wear white because the color white was the symbol of wealth. Her courtiers thought she was crazy for wanting to wear white on her wedding day. But she was the queen, and that is the rest of the story.

Finally, where did all our present wedding vows come from? Sorry to be the bearer of such bad news, but they didn't come from the Bible (although the sentiment did). They all came from the Church of England. And who is the head of the Church of England?—the British monarch, until this very day.

So if you think that husbands and wives should sleep in the same bed, that young brides should wear white, and you have a crease down the front and rear of your pants, you are simple mimicking British royalty.

CHAPTER **3**

# The Church's Historical Stand on Sex Through the Ages

**We will never understand the teachings of biblical Christianity until we understand that the Bible is not primarily a text on how to live the Christian life but is primarily a book of basic principles by which we live the Christian life.**

Many men were counted as righteous long before there was any law or rules on telling us how we should live. Enoch walked with God and did not die but was taken straight to heaven (Genesis 5:24).

Noah was the only righteous man that God could find at the time and so was instructed by God on how to build the ark and save a male and female of all living creatures (Genesis 6:9–10).

Abraham simply believed God when the angel told him he would be the father of many nations even when he was one hundred years old, and his wife, Sarah, was ninety. Because of this, God counted him as righteous, and he has been rightly called the "father of the righteous" (Romans 4:3).

Isaac, Jacob, Joseph, Moses, Gideon, Caleb, Daniel, and the prophets were all godly men. David was called "a man after God's own heart" (1 Samuel 13:14).

The rules that Christians live by came a long time after there were righteous and godly men on the earth. One might think that before God created humanity that he would set the rules of the game of life up first. But he didn't. The rules came about two thousand years later. Jesus hit the nail on the head when the rich young ruler asked about the greatest commandment: love. "On this hang all the laws and rules and commandments" (Mark 12:30–31). He further explained what this meant to the young man who had asked what the most important commandment was, after which Jesus told him the story of the Good Samaritan.

All of the Mosaic law and the Ten Commandments are simply pointers to what it means to love God and neighbor. All the teachings of Jesus and Paul are doing the same thing.

At the core of man's being is the desire to find justification through works. Even though we give verbal ascent and teach salvation by faith, at the core of our being, there is still this compulsion to earn our salvation by being good enough. It is from this condition of man that gives birth to our craving and desire for laws and rules.

In light of this condition, God chose to spell out some specifics, which He gave with the Ten Commandments and the Mosaic law.

When Jesus came along, the law given by Moses had become so corrupted that Jesus was repulsed by it. Hence His statement about love and His anger at the money changers in the temple. The Jews, at one time in their history, had been completely conquered by the Persians. After a few hundred years, through the intervention and leadership of Nehemiah, the Persians allowed the Jews to return to their native lands as long as they submitted to Persian rule.

The Jews knew that the only reason they had been abandoned by God in the first place was because they had turned their hearts from Him, had not kept His laws and precepts, and had worshipped foreign gods. They therefore decided that the best thing they could do to ensure such a humiliation would never happen again was to expand on the Mosaic law and make laws for every conceivable area of human existence. They called this the Talmud. This is why, in Jesus's time, the term "rabbi," meaning teacher and "teachers of the law," were used constantly.

As a Christian living in a Western civilization, we live by two sets of laws.

1.  Civic law. If we have a question with civic law, we go and seek advice or guidance from a lawyer or attorney who are experts in civic law.
2.  Christian law. However, as a Christian, we also try to live by Christian laws, which are not covered by civic law; and therefore we go and seek advice, or guidance, from a cler-gyperson, who is supposed to be an expert in Christian law, to make sure we make Christian decisions.

However, in Jewish society, the two were one and the same. There was only one law, and this was Jewish law; and the teachers and lawyers had spent several hundreds of years putting it together. It still exists to this day.

Let me give you three examples:

1.  Rape. Of course the law condemned rape. But what is rape? By this, I mean, even to this day, we have lawsuits around the consensual aspect of rape. Now from a rational point of view, it's a simple matter. Sexual relations between two consenting adults is not rape. But if one is not consensual, it is rape.

    But here comes the dilemma. Other than the two peo-ple involved, who knows if it was consensual or not? The rabbis and lawyers needed an answer to this dilemma by coming up with a simple answer: "If no one heard the girl scream, it was not rape. But if anyone heard her scream, it was rape." Problem solved. Next.
2.  Working on the Sabbath. The Ten Commandments say that we are not to work on the Sabbath day. But what constitutes work? Without going into all the intricacies of

what constituted work, let's just look at one aspect: travel. Is going on a long journey work? According to the writers of the Talmud, that depends on the length of the journey. So they set the distance at about half a mile. This is why we have references to a Sabbath-day's journey in the gospels.

However, we now have a further problem, half a mile from where or what? While the Jews changed this several times, they eventually decided that it was to be half a mile from one's home. But what constitutes your home, your house maybe? But what if you had a shack at the far end of your property that you often overnighted in? Could that also be called your home? So finally, what they settled on was that it had to be half a mile from where there was food that you had prepared.

Enterprising Jews soon found ways around a seemingly simple solution so that they could travel without restriction. What if you were a Jew, and you needed to go on a journey that would take you more than half a mile? You wanted to set out on the Sabbath at, say, midday to make it by the following evening, but it is beyond a Sabbath-day's journey.

The answer was simple and legal. You set out on the Sabbath day and traveled half a mile, to the extent of a Sabbath-day's journey, and there you lay a piece of food that you have prepared under a tree or bury it where you could recover it on the return trip. Now you can go for another Sabbath-day's journey and repeat the procedure until the Sabbath was over, or you ran out of food. Then you could keep traveling without restriction for a whole week, whereby you would need to prepare more food to hide or simply drop on the ground.

**Jesus tried to bring balance with His teaching on love.**

However, by the time the early church came around, the pendulum had swung the completely opposite direction with many Christians wanting to throw the law out completely. So now, along came Paul who tried to again rebalance the issues and thereby gave us a whole lot of laws and rules to help us do what God intended us to do in the first place, which was to live our lives according to the law of love.

The next two thousand years became a time of the church, rocking from side to side with the sides today being labeled liberalism and conservatism, or more correctly, legalism.

So to put it in a nutshell, we could safely say the following: "Every law stated by God, Moses, Jesus, and Paul were attempts to penetrate our dark and sinful hearts to bring enlightenment to what it meant to live by the law of love as Paul told the church at Corinth." "The letter of the law kills, but the spirit of the law gives life" (2 Corinthians 3:6). Furthermore, it was never God's intention for the Bible to be the complete text on how to live out this law on love or how to live the Christian life.

If it were, we would never have the condoning of slavery in the Bible by Moses, Jesus, and Paul. So to maintain that the teaching of the Bible is complete on how to live the specifics of the Christian life is completely false. This is not to suggest that any teaching in the Bible on how we are to live is wrong, but it is an acknowledgment that the instructions are neither inclusive nor conclusive of all Christian living for all cultures in all times and ages. In essence, when it comes to how to live a Christian life, the Bible is a book of timeless and unchanging principles, not of specifics, that would need to be adjusted with the ebb and flow of cultures and times.

Another classic example of this absurd literalism is the often-heard expression that "God raises up and puts down kings and rulers and that every leader that is raised up is raised up by God" (Romans 13:1–5). The strange thing is, the only time I have ever heard that expression was when a Republican was in the White House. The fact is that God didn't raise up Trump, Obama, Bush, Lincoln, Washington, Hitler, or any other ruler for that matter. The people raised them all up, or in some cases, they raised themselves up. When the Bible talks about God raising up kings and rulers, He is meaning that the principle of orderly government is ordained by God so that we can all live out our lives of love to God and each other and that anarchy and chaos will not reign.

To believe that God raises up certain individuals to places of leadership in various countries would mean that God was to blame for the genocide of the North American native peoples, the Holocaust, and the wholesale slaughter of approximately one hundred million people in world wars I and II and the twenty million Christians murdered by the Communists in the Bolshevik Revolution.

I use these topics as a way of illustrating the absurdity of taking statements from the Bible out of context and cultural understanding and endeavoring to apply them to our Christian lives in a modern world.

With this in mind, let's look at the church's stated position on sex down through the ages. It seems that, like the Jews of old, it too has been whittle down to details of sexual activity and nuances to something that could be put in a sexual Talmud. Simple laws for everyone to obey and therefore solve all sexual problems forever.

Let's see how they did.

**Thomas Aquinas** was a great man of God in the Middle Ages. However, he also claimed that fornication was having sex with one's wife for enjoyment rather than for bearing children. The church also taught that if man looked at his wife with thoughts of having sex with her, other than to have children, that he had to go to confession to be absolved of his sin. If a man or woman enjoyed sex with their spouse, they had sinned, and they had to go to confession for absolution. It was okay to be raped as long as you didn't enjoy it. If you enjoyed it, you too had to go to confession.

Hannelie Wood of the University of South Africa said the follow regarding the teaching of the church fathers on the subjects of women and sexuality:

**Jerome**, a Christian apologist, held Eve and, as a consequence, every woman responsible for all heresy (Keane 1987:3). Jerome viewed woman as the root of all evil (cited in Phelips 1931:203).

**Chrysostom** in his homily 1X (1843) contended that because Eve sinned, all women were punished with subjection. He wrote that woman [Eve] taught once and ruined all, for the sex is weak and fickle; and he was speaking of the sex collectively.

Although **Clement of Alexandria** accepted the reality of sex, he advocated that it is only to fulfill God's will for procreation. He denounced and condemned physical pleasure as well as the femaleness of women (Ide 1984).

**Tertullian**, as cited in Ide (1984:75–78), stated in his *Prescription Against Heretics* that only men are created in the image of God and that they were innocent victims of the "wiles and evils of women."

**Origen** disapproved of the sexual act even within marriage (Phelips 1931:203). Weinrich (1991:258) states that Origen described women as "worse than animals" because of their constant state of lust (Keane 1987:12; Vogt 2003:59).

For **Tertullian**, women were the source of evil, and he believed that there was nothing good about women in general or any woman in particular. In his view, women were responsible for pain, suffering, sin, and corruption (Tavard 1973:58–59). Tertullian despised women so much that he warned man against gazing upon them because it would mean that they would have their immortal souls consigned to hell and would be doomed to never enjoy the security of heaven after death (Tavard 1973:59).

**Jerome** viewed women as the root of all evil. He declared that a clean body signifies a dirty mind because he found all aspects of sexuality repugnant (Strachan and Strachan 1958:6). Jerome claimed that although virginity is better because men are corrupted through sexual intercourse (Ide1984:72).

**Augustine,** in his views on the natural order, states in the *Heptateuch* that women were created with a weaker brain.

**Chrysostom** described women as weak and flighty, a fault of nature, evil, as temptresses, and as mischievous (Knight 1974:121). Among all the savage beasts, none is found to be so harmful as women. The whole of her body is nothing less than phlegm, blood, bile, and the fluid of digested food (cited in Cooper-White 2012:72).

**In conclusion,** the church fathers left the carnal woman in an ontological state as lustful temptresses and, for example;

**Tertullian** in his *Apparel of Women* (1951:117) could refer to women as the "devils gateway."

David Instone-Brewer said the following: "[**Augustine**] regarded sex as inherently sinful (perhaps because of his misspent youth, a time in which he uttered his famous prayer, "Grant me chastity and continence but not yet.").

Sex was prohibited on the following days:

1. Sunday, as it was the Lord's day
2. Thursdays and Fridays, in preparation for Communion
3. During Lent, which could be forty-seven to sixty-two days
4. In preparation for Christmas for thirty-five days
5. Pentecost for forty to sixty days
6. Various feast days

Oral sex was forbidden along with masturbation. The missionary position was the only one that was allowed due to the fact that it was the least pleasurable, and it enabled the male to be dominant.

**Thomas Aquinas** taught that excessive sex shortened one's life, diminished the physique, weakened the mental ability, and impaired insight.

**Augustine** taught that a man who loves his wife too much is also an adulterous.

These were the views, beliefs, teachings, preaching, and writings of the church fathers concerning women and sexuality. As our young people today would say, "This is all messed up, man." To which I would add, "That has got to be the understatement of the year."

What makes this all the more repugnant and difficult to believe is that these theologians, bishops, archbishops, scholars, and church leaders were reading the very same Bible that we use today, albeit in a different language. They were only a few hundred years from the actual time of Christ. Furthermore, approximately half of them were beautified by the Church as saints.

So this begs the question, "How could these men be so blind?"

The reason is that they were interpreting the scriptures through their paradigm of the prevailing culture of the day, which was a powerful influence created by the Greek philosophers Plato and Aristotle. It was a culture that dehumanized and degraded women.

Still we would ask, "How could they be so blind?" Which of course brings us to the very situation of sexuality in the church today. All the scriptures regarding women and sexuality are viewed through the prism of the interpretation of church history regarding these subjects. This means that we are no different in our blindness, on these issues, as were the church fathers. As Solomon said, "There is nothing new under the sun" (Ecclesiastes 1:9).

It would be easy to dismiss the relevance of the statements of these church leaders as simply the opinions of some ill-informed individuals of nearly two thousand years ago. However, to do so would be a grave mistake. Their sentiments expressed by theses church leaders regarding women and sexuality are the foundations upon which the present church convictions and teachings on the subject are built. Many evangelical fundamentalist Christians of today are perpetuating those same disgusting sentiments expressed by the early church leaders.

A writer for the British Broadcasting Corporation Future, Brandon Ambrosino, said, "It was the stoics who, attempting to curb self-indulgence, tried to fit sex into a scheme of meaning: indulging in the pleasure of sex was all right as long as it was for the purposes of making babies. This ethic worked its way into Christian tradition, famously through Augustine, and continues to weld enormous influence in the West. According to this framework, sex is ethical when it is practiced promisingly for procreation. (To clarify, though this is presented as a Christian ethic, its origin lies elsewhere. In fact, the biblical book of Song of Solomon celebrates wild, passionate, erotic sex on its own terms between two lovers, not between husband and wife, as later Christian commentators wrongly interpreted the poem.)"

Perhaps one of the most powerful pieces of evidence as to the ineptness and ignorance of the leaders of the Christian church regarding their teaching on biblical sexuality is portrayed in the story of Catherine of Aragon and King Henry VIII of England.

King Henry's father was Henry VII and had made a peace treaty with Spain. To seal the treaty, as was the custom in those days, they agreed that Catherine of Aragon, the daughter of the Spanish queen, would marry Henry VIII's son, Prince Arthur.

Catherine went to London and married Prince Arthur in 1501, and all was well between England and Spain. However, Prince Arthur was not a strong person physically and died five months later. Catherine claimed that due to Arthur's ill health, he had not consummated the marriage, and the debate on the subject continues to this day. Consequently, she fell in love with Arthur's younger brother, Henry, and they wanted to get married. However, they needed to get the pope's blessing and permission.

Now this situation was the very situation that the Bible is referencing in Deuteronomy 25:5 where it says, "When a married man dies, his brother is to go and have sex with his brother's widow so that she may have children." The Bible also says that if he doesn't want to marry her, he must take her to the city father's at the city gates and tell them that he does not want to marry her. She is then to spit in his face and slap him with a sandal for being such a terrible person. Only then is she free to marry someone else. However, in this story, Henry and Catherine wanted to get married, which would be in perfect accordance with the biblical teaching on the subject. It was God's way of ensuring that widows and orphans would be cared for.

Unfortunately, it would seem that neither the pope nor any biblical scholar in either Rome or London had ever read that section of the Bible but had zeroed in on a completely different section where God said in Leviticus 20:21 that "it was an abomination for a man to have sex with his brother's wife." It seems that no one had enough sense or perception to realize that the verse in Deuteronomy was referring to a situation of when a man died, and the reference in Leviticus was when a man was living, which would be adultery.

And so at first, the pope would not allow the marriage. It was only after eight years that Catherine was able to convince the pope that her marriage with Arthur had not been consummated that he gave permission for them to be married. You may be asking, "What has that got to do with the biblical teaching of sex?"

The point is that none of those ignorant priests, monks, biblical scholars, bishops, cardinals, theologians, popes, and kings had a clue about what the Bible taught about sex. They simply cherry-picked the verses from the Bible that supported their own ignorant and arrogant prejudices and then had the audacity to make laws regarding sex and marriage that have extended down to this very day.

However, here is a further subtle twist to this story. The pope and all the church guys in Rome *would* have been aware of the first reference in Deuteronomy. How do we know this? Because the Christian church at that time was split into two churches, East and West. The Western church was ruled from Rome and the Eastern church was ruled from Constantinople, now Istanbul in Turkey. The Eastern church acknowledged and practiced the same interpretation that I have just referred to above. So why did the Western church in Rome insist on this erroneous teaching? I think I have a very accurate idea.

After spending most of my adult life as a pastor in the church, I will guarantee that the West held to this strict erroneous interpretation purely as a political act of piety. I can hear the conversations now, "We are not liberals like the Eastern church. We must hold to the pure truth of God's Word. God said it, I believe it, that's good enough for me. We are holy, more righteous, and more Christian than they are. Once we start down this slippery slope, who can tell where we will end up?"

I believe that this was the breeding ground for the wrong teaching of biblical sexuality that has been propagated over the last few hundred years and finally wound up as the purity culture. There is no way that we could possibly comprehend the incredible damage that has been done to possibly millions of people who were in love and were not able to express their love because of this false teaching of the Christian church.

But the greatest damage of all is that because of this false, non-biblical teaching, millions have also rejected the church and the message of redemption through Jesus Christ. The demise of the church since WWII has not been because people decided to live sinful lives but is in large part due to this outrageous false teaching that the church has propagated regarding sex.

The church has brought destruction upon itself. The church not only used its power and influence to repress sexual expression and activity but also for financial gain. The reason priests are not allowed to marry has nothing to do with being kept separate from the world. In ancient times, a man's wealth would go to his oldest son upon his death. This is called "primogeniture" and is still prevalent in England until this very day. The church then came up with the idea that if they decreed that the oldest son should be a priest, he was in fact marrying the church. This would result in his inheritance going to the church upon his father's death. This is how the Roman Catholic Church acquired such great wealth.

This was not meant to be any kind of restriction on his sexual activity as he was free to have sex with whoever he wished and to raise children. As time went on however, the church decided that it would be better if priests were celibate.

After the reformation, the Anglican Church in England decreed that a man could not leave his wealth to his son if he was born out of wedlock. This was because, at the time, it was estimated that 80 percent of all brides were pregnant at the time of their wedding.

When I grew up, the big sexual sin was masturbation. At Christian youth camps, all the boys would be taken to a meeting of just men, while a Christian medical doctor lectured us on the evils of "'self-abuse." He told us that it would stunt our growth and that we would be impotent by the time we were thirty-five years of age. I remember going to the dictionary to find out what "impotent" meant. I also remember thinking how irrelevant that was, as twenty years away was like another lifetime.

In the midseventies, Dr. James Dobson of Focus on the Family declared that masturbation was no big deal and not a sin unless it became an obsession. However, it wasn't long before the church was at it again; but of course now, the field is narrowing. Premarital sex is so accepted that it doesn't get a mention anymore. All this leaves us with now is lust and pornography. So let's look at both of these from a scriptural perspective.

CHAPTER 4

# WHAT IS LUST?

Several years ago, I attended a men's retreat put on by the church I attended. The speaker was some expert on "men's issues," and so it was supposed to be enlightening. The whole retreat was nothing more than the speaker berating good Christian men for their struggle with lust and sexual desire.

I remember the speaker made this statement: "When I got off the plane to come to this retreat, I saw a beautiful woman. I kept walking. But if I had looked again, it would have been lust." I was so angry I nearly walked out of the session but decided to stay and see what other stupid statements he would make. I was not disappointed. He made many of them. I wanted to stand up and tell him to get lost and stop bringing guilt and condemnation upon Christian men for simply being human.

Let me put it straight and plain. For a man to be attracted by a beautiful woman is not lust. That's how God made us. For a man to be sexually attracted by a beautiful or sexy woman is not lust. That's how God made us. For a man to admire her sexuality is not lust. It is the way God made us. For a man to contemplate what it would be like to have sex with the woman is not lust. It's the way God made us.

If you are a man reading this, stop feeling guilty or condemned for being attracted to beautiful and sexy women and having a desire to have sex with them. All those desires were put there by God for two reasons. One reason is so you would propagate the human race. The second is that you would enjoy sexual pleasures. Without these desires and instincts, humanity would have become an extinct species millions of years ago. All these things do is prove that you're a normal male made by God in order to procreate. In fact, some anthropologist believe that men were made with a "wandering eye" so as to combat incest.

However, that is not the end of the story. God not only gave us these natural sexual instincts, but he also made us moral creatures created in His image so that our instincts, which were given for pro-creation and physical enjoyment purposes, would be tempered and held in balance in order to bring harmony and respect for all people, both male and female. To give vent to our natural sexual instincts is to degrade ourselves to the level of animals. But to unjustly bind our instincts is to rob us of one of the great joys that God has given us.

Obviously, what we are striving for is a healthy balance between these two extremes. This balancing act is only made possible by the direction and power of the Holy Spirit. However, if Christian history has taught us anything, it has taught us that man would rather create and live by laws and rules that can be mandated and articulated, as the Jews did with the Talmud, rather than through the presence and direction of the Holy Spirit in our lives.

### Lust is not sexual desire.

So what is lust? Lust is not sexual desire. The word lust in the church today has come to denote sexual desire because of the false teaching and preaching of many pastors on the subject.

The word "lust" simply means a compelling desire to the point of obsession. This was what God was referring to in the tenth commandment when He said that we should not covet. You will remember that He listed several things, including another man's possessions and his wife.

The most authoritative source of the meaning of any English word is the *Oxford Dictionary*. This is how "lust" is defined in the *Oxford Collocations Dictionary*:

> **Lust (lust for something)—very strong desire for something or enjoyment of something to satisfy his lust for power. She has a real lust for life (= she really enjoys life).**

Notice that there is not one single reference or even anything suggesting a sexual connection in any way, shape, or form.

Likewise, the original Greek word used here simply means "desire." While coveting your neighbor's wife may involve sexual desires, it's unlikely that coveting a neighbor's house or field is sexual in nature. And in most New Testament uses, the word does not have a clear sexual connotation.

Below are four different ways that the same Greek word for lust is translated into English in **bold print.**

1. *For truly, I say to you, many prophets and righteous people* **longed to see what you see,** *and did not see it, and to hear what you hear, and did not hear it* (Matthew 13:17 ESV).
2. *And he said to them,* **"I have earnestly desired** *to eat this Passover with you before I suffer"* (Luke 22:15 ESV).
3. **I coveted no one's** *silver or gold or apparel* (Acts 20:33 ESV).
4. *And he was* **longing** *to be fed with the pods that the pigs ate, and no one gave him anything* (Luke 15:16 ESV).

So we see in these four examples that the Greek word for lust can be interpreted as longed, earnestly desired, coveted, and longing.

According to Wikipedia, "Lust is an emotion or feeling of intense desire in the body. The lust can take any form such as the lust for knowledge, the lust for sex or the lust for power. It can take such mundane forms as the lust for food as distinct from the need for food. Lust is a powerful psychological force producing intense wanting for an object, or circumstance fulfilling the emotion."

Sexual desire, in and of itself, is not lust. Sexual desire can become lust but so can desire for anything, including a house, car, money, or success. We often hear women say that they saw something that "was to die for." That's lust—pure and simple. Our sexual desires, instincts, and search for sexual gratification were made and ordained by God. Just because I admire a beautiful car does not mean that I want to commit sin and steal it. Just because I have a need for money does not mean that I would rob a bank and take it. Just because I admire a beautiful and sexy woman and may even be mesmerized by her beauty does not mean that I want to commit adultery with her. The issue is what we do with the attraction. Do we savor and toy with it until it becomes an obsession, which is lust, or do we simply admire, appreciate, and move on?

I am reminded of a story I read many years ago of a British Army chaplain who was captured along with his unit by the Nazis in World War II. The Nazis wanted to get military information from him but decide that because he was a man of God that they would not torture him to make him talk. They decided therefore to test his spiritual resolve and thereby humiliated him in the hope that he would break and give them the information they needed. They stripped him naked and tied him on his back to a bed in a small room. After a short time, an interrogator came in. She was a woman—beautiful, sexy, and naked. She introduced herself and sat down on the bed next to him and began to interrogate him. Of course, it wasn't too long before he had an erection. This was exactly what the interrogator wanted. She used his erection in order to berate him and condemn him and asked him how he could call himself a man of God by letting himself get an erection. I think his response was priceless. He said, "Don't you think that, under these circumstances, the Almighty would think that an erection would be a perfectly normal reaction?"

It may help if you are a man and have felt guilty when you have been drawn to look at a beautiful woman or some sensual picture that "under the circumstances, the Almighty would think that your desire to look, be drawn to, and appreciate would be a perfectly normal reaction?"

I find it incredibly ironical that a woman can spend two hours each day making herself beautiful and sexually attractive, but if a man (heaven forbid) happens to notice her, he is a perverted sicko dealing with lust.

Furthermore, if her husband or boyfriend happens to notice another woman that has also spent two hours making herself attractive, it becomes tantamount to a death wish.

If you are a woman reading this, you really need to think long and hard about what I just said. However, I must, in all fairness, say that just as God gave man an instinct to look out for beautiful women in order to enjoy sex and procreate, He also gave woman the same instinct that makes them want to spend two hours in the bathroom every morning, trying to make themselves as attractive as possible. That too is a God-given instinct.

So, ladies, lighten up on the guys. If it is wrong for men to notice attractive women, then it's equally wrong for you to make yourself attractive in order for men to notice you. Conversely, if it is okay for you to make yourself attractive, then it goes without saying that it is okay for your man to notice other women who have also made themselves attractive. A typical response from a woman to this statement would be that she feels threatened by him noticing other women and that she thinks he wants to have the other woman instead of her.

Let me put this in perspective. What would you think if your man got mad that you were making yourself look attractive each morning because it made him feel that you were trying to attract other men to yourself and didn't want him? Another illustration would be that most women are attracted to babies. Does that mean they want to disown their own children and take the baby home? Of course not. They are attracted to babies because that's the way God made them.

However, in all fairness, I need to point out that it really isn't the woman's fault. It is in fact a result of the curse God put upon her because of Eve's sin.

When Adam and Eve sinned in the Garden of Eden, God pronounced several curses upon them. Man would have to work by the sweat of his brow to make a living and pull weeds from the ground. Eve's curse was that she would have great pain in childbearing and that her "desire would be for her husband" (Genesis 3:16).

For many years I couldn't figure out how a woman "desiring her husband" would be a punishment and a curse. Surely, that would be a good thing. Until eventually, the penny dropped, and I got the picture. What God was saying is that the woman's curse would be that she would be obsessed by her husband and live in mortal fear of losing him.

You see, guys, it isn't really their fault personally. It's in their DNA, and they can't really help it. I think, once we realize what causes this rage in a woman, it will help us understand it and be more loving (like Christ loved the church) and accommodating.

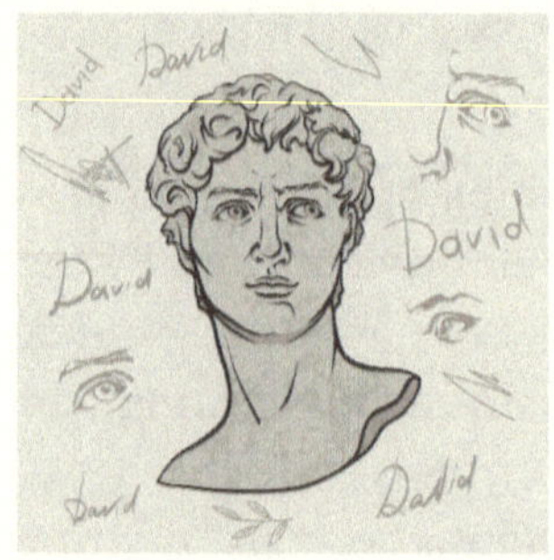



CHAPTER 5

# NAKEDNESS

While it may seem presumptuous to assume that the church and the world sank into the Dark Ages because of its cubing of sexual pleasure, there is no denying that the expression of sexual pleasure was at the forefront of the Renaissance. The Renaissance started in Florence, Italy. And if there is one thing that every tourist wants to see in Florence, it is Michael Angelo's naked statue of David.

There is absolutely no denying that there is a direct corelation between free sexual expression and an enlightened and educated society on the one hand and an ignorant society along with sexual repression on the other.

With regard to sexuality, I firmly believe that the conservative Christian church of today is still in the Dark Ages with respect to its teachings and behaviors that have absolutely no scriptural foundation at all but in essence are contrary to biblical teaching.

No matter how long we look at the subject, we cannot get away from the fact that it was God's original intention for us all to be naked. Yes, Adam and Eve sinned, and God turned them out of the Garden of Eden and pronounced curses upon them.

1. Men would have to pull weeds from the ground and earn a living by the sweat of their brow.
2. Women would have great pain in childbearing.
3. Women would be obsessed with their husbands and experience insecurity because of it.
4. Women would have their husbands rule over them.
5. Both had their relationship with God broken.
6. Both were driven out of the Garden of Eden
7. Both would eventually die.

It is interesting to note that apart from the universal curse of death for all mankind, the broken relationship with God, and being banished from the Garden of Eden, only one punishment was for Adam but three for Eve. We'll look at this again later. What is interesting is the issue of nakedness. By sinning, they became aware of their nakedness, and God clothed them. However, it is abundantly evident that clothing was never God's intention. In fact, God clothed them with the skins of animals, which tells us that the very first deaths that took place were because of their shame.

Having God make clothes for Adam and Eve was not a punishment or a curse but an obvious act of kindness to help them cope with this new revelation that they had never experienced before, called shame. But we need to ask ourselves, what was the source of the shame? I am indebted to Nadia Bolz-Weber's thought in her book *Shameless: A Sexual Reformation* that shame for our nakedness did not come from God.

Adam said that they were naked and ashamed, and God responded with, "Who told you you were naked" (Genesis 3:3)?

So if it wasn't God who told them they were naked and needed to be ashamed, who was it? There was only one other entity present, and that was Satan. It is obvious that the serpent tempted Eve, and immediately, after she and Adam had eaten the fruit, he accused them of being naked and shamed them. So the shame that we have of our nakedness does not come from God; it comes from the serpent.

We have seven judgments or curses, one for men, three for women, and three are universal. Let's take a look and see what we have done with these seven judgments since that day forward.

1. Man has eternally sought to find an easier way to earn a living other than by the sweat of his brow.
2. Women have, since the beginning of time, done everything possible to reduce the pain of childbirth.
3. Women have struggled to control the jealousy against other women because of their marital insecurity.
4. Universally, we have believed that a man was to rule over his wife, but it certainly didn't get Paul's endorsement when he told husbands to love their wives as Christ loved the church (Ephesians 5:25). That would rule out a husband ruling over his wife.
5. Universally, man has done everything in his power to ward off death.
6. All religions in the world are expressions of man's attempt to find the relationship that Adam and Eve had with God.
7. We have endeavored to create lives that are as close as possible to the Garden of Eden. Some even go to great lengths to create little Garden of Edens in their yards. And if we can't do that, we take vacations and visit paradisaical places that could very well be like the Garden of Eden. We adorn the walls of our homes with pictures of beautiful scenes of nature to remind us of where we really belong. This ancient paradise, which was where we all began, calls us to return home. This calling is universal within all mankind, and it calls from deep within our soul.

As you can see, we, as a human race, have done everything possible to reverse the effect or the curse of sin and return to the Garden of Eden. There would not be a rational Christian anywhere who would say that by endeavoring to reverse the effects of the seven curses that we are doing anything wrong or sinful. On the contrary, most would agree that it is admirable and perfectly natural.

What then is the big hang-up with nakedness? It was God's intention that we enjoy this paradise and to also enjoy our nakedness. God never condemned nakedness, nor did he command Adam and Eve to wear clothes. More to the point is that the issue of ours is one of shame.

Many people still seem to be suffering from the shame of their nakedness and have never looked at the possibility that God wanted us to be naked in the first place.

Just as sex was God's idea, so was nakedness. Have you ever noticed that young children have no shame of their nakedness? We teach them that it is shameful.

**I choose to believe that it is shameful to teach our children that the things that God intended to be beautiful are to be covered up and considered shameful.**

Children seem to have an innate sense about what is fair or right and wrong but universally don't seem to have any shame about their nakedness. Furthermore, it seems to be even more interesting that they are not ashamed of their nakedness even when everyone else is wearing clothes. I also find it very interesting to note that it is only certain types of nakedness that seem to be unacceptable, while other forms are not only acceptable but admired and commendable.

Several years ago, I was with a group of college students in an art gallery. One of the young ladies came to me and said, "I just realized that this is an art gallery full of statues of naked people." I acknowledge that her observation was correct. However, what I wanted to say, but didn't because it would not have been appropriate, was this: "Yes, but what I can't understand is that for us to look at all this and consider it educational and culturally enlightening and our viewing of it is encouraged by our society. But if we looked at photographs or paintings in a book or a magazine of naked people, we would be accused of viewing pornography. And if we were looking at real naked people, we would all be called sick perverts by that very same society. But, hey, it's all A-okay as they are only made of marble.

So that makes it all perfectly acceptable and commendable, even in conservative Christian circles."

Several years ago, I had an appointment with a man who would be the equivalent of a bishop in the denomination that I was with. His office was in his home. And when I knocked on the front door, his wife came and invited me in. She explained that he was held up on a phone call and invited me into their living room and offered me cookies and coffee. As we sat together, I tried to make some small talk and asked her what she liked to do in her spare time. She said that she loved reading. This raised my interest as I am also an avid reader. And so I asked her what types of books she liked to read. To my utmost shock, I found that she devoured Mills & Boon books and other romance novels. It appeared that was all she read.

Apart from the fact that her reading could barely qualify for what most of us mean by reading, it took me all my powers of self-control to not ask the following question by saying, "So I guess if you love reading about the fantasy of a romance where people continually have affairs and sexual encounters that you find alluring and entertaining. I would assume that you have no problem with your husband subscribing to *Playboy* or *Penthouse* magazines."

As I reflect back, I wish I had said it. I find it difficult to understand why preachers and other church leaders can preach against pornography when their wives are reading novels of fantasy sexual relations. There is absolutely no difference. The same truth holds for women who are addicted to soap operas where there is continual cheating and sexual activity in the story line.

I come back to this very basic issue that it was clearly God's intent for us to be naked and never wear clothes. I would also point out that, of all the curses that God extended to mankind because of his sin in the Garden of Eden, universally, man has endeavored to remove their effects and live as God intended us to live. However, God never cursed us with clothing, nor did He even command us to wear clothing; and yet it seems that we want to rain down curses on anyone, particularly men, who want to look at a picture of a naked women.

Am I suggesting that in an endeavor to be holy, as God intended, we should all burn our clothes and run around naked? Certainly not. The sight would be repulsive. What I am saying is that there is nothing sinful or wrong with looking at pictures of naked people of both sexes.

It's interesting to note that in the United States, the Christian church has a very large influence and presence, considerably more than any other Western country. The United States also has the strictest censorship in the Western world with regard to nudity on TV.

Isn't it ironical, therefore, that the United States is more obsessed with sex than any other country in the Western world?

This definitely proves the old adage that "forbidden fruit is the sweetest." I firmly believe that our shame of our bodies is induced by our culture. What is interesting to note is that not all cultures consider covering the same parts of the body. There are several cultures in the world where there is nothing shameful about a woman going topless, even to church. Other cultures insist on women covering their faces and still others where women will wear nothing over their breasts but will always cover their shoulders.

It seems to be incredibly strange to me that mankind should be mandated by law, religion, and culture to cover something that God never originally intended to be covered.

I had to laugh when I read what Nadia Bolz-Weber said: "I've noticed that the less integrated physically, emotionally, and spiritually someone is, the more pornography they tend to consume. This is anecdotal evidence and not a scientific study. Nevertheless,

**I'd like to congratulate conservative Christians on their success in bolstering an industry that they claim to despise."**

I believe that the wearing of clothes and the covering of our genitalia came about because of very practical purposes.

    a)    The need to be warm or to protect ourselves from the sun

b)   The covering of our genitalia developed as a natural protection of the most sensitive parts of our bodies. Have you ever watched the TV program *Naked and Afraid?*

Here we have two people of the opposite sex appearing on worldwide television totally naked and yet without any reservations or embarrassment. And yet, within two days, they have made protection for their genitalia in order to protect them in the outdoor environment. It would certainly be the most natural thing to do.

c)   Military combat. Of all the areas of a man's body that he would want to protect in combat, it would be his genitals.
d)   Adornment. How else can a person show to the world that they rank above others than by the clothing they wear?

The ancient Hawaiians never wore any clothes; and in fact, it was against the law to do so. Only the royal families were allowed to wear clothing as a sign of their rank and status among their people. Anybody else wearing clothing would be accused of being uppity and putting on airs and would be severely punished. The ancient Greek Olympians would all appear for their games totally naked for the opening ceremonies and then tie their genitals up with a loin cloth so they wouldn't be harmed in the particular sport they were engaged in. There are many cultures in European history where all individuals swim and bathe naked.

It would seem, therefore, that the present prudish attitude regarding the naked body, particularly in the United States, is not only quite extraordinary but totally senseless.

# CHAPTER 6

# POLYGAMY

Writer for the British Broadcasting Corporation Earth, Melissa Hogenboom, puts it well when she said, "Love has always been the same, right? A man falls for a woman, they get married, pop out a few children, and stay together in a harmonious and monogamous relationship for life."

Sorry, romantics. This wasn't and still isn't always the picture of love. Polygamy, where more than one spouse is allowed, was the norm for many of our hunter-gatherer ancestors and flourished when our ancestors began to settle down. A preference for it then appears to have arisen, among many other reasons, for economic purposes.

It made it easier for fathers to divide and share valuable commodities, such as land, with their children. Monogamy later got hijacked by romantic love by idealistic nineteenth century Victorians. "The idea of sexual exclusivity started emerging fairly late in the game," said professor of law Hadar Aviram at UC Hastings College of the Law in San Francisco, US. Even today, monogamy is the minority relationship style around the world.

**"Cultural estimates suggest that as many as 83 percent of societies around the world allow polygamy."**

It would be easy to suspect that the church had something to do with the change from polygamy to monogamy. It didn't, well at least not in the beginning. In fact, the church had nothing to do with it until around AD 750.

The church was the final hold out against monogamy, but finally capitulated and made it mandatory. As Christianity was built on Judaism, and Judaism was polygamous, they were in fact some of the very last to change and finally surrendered to the liberal trends all around it. Some have thought that it was Paul's statement that "a deacon should only have one wife." But not only is this an incorrect translation of what he said, but it defiantly had nothing to do with the gigantic sea change in societies within the Greek and Roman Empires from being polygamous to monogamous. The Greeks were well on their way to becoming monogamous three hundred years before Christ. What caused this? While there may have been several causes, there was one particular one that helped bring about the change.

This has to do with the Greek and Roman Empires. They were not the first civilizations to develop huge invading armies. Before them were others, such as the Egyptians and Genghis Khan, but they were nothing compared with the armies of the Greeks and the Romans. What do great armies need more than anything else?—simple answer: an inexhaustible supply of dedicated soldiers. But how does a warlord or great general acquire these men?

Let's understand the picture. In today's world, most of the western world lives in basically egalitarian societies. This was not so for thousands of years. They had the filthy rich and the poor (the masses). The rich had three things: money, land, and wives. Now if you were one of the poor men, you had no money, and you had no land. This means that there was no way you could ever afford a wife. And even if you could, they were virtually all taken by the wealthy polygamists. Not only that, but the rich got out of military service by paying for the wars, while the poor fought and died in the wars.

Somewhere, at some time in history, a warlord had an epiphany, and the word got out that if men would join his army, he would allow them to have a wife and live at the army base. But where were all those women going to come from?—from the people that they conquered. When an army was formed, they marched into the towns, and the conquering leaders took the loot and the land, and the fighting soldiers took the women and some of the loot. In order for us to understand how this massive sea change from polygamy to monogamy happened, we need to go back further in history than the Greeks and realize that up, until then, the marauding raiders such as the Egyptians, Genghis Khan, and others simply plundered, murdered, raped, pillaged, and razed to the ground and then moved on to do it all again. This was not only true of all major invaders before the Greeks but also of the Vandals and Vikings and others for approximately 1,500 years after the Roman Empire had fallen. Now I know that marauding armies have always pillaged, raped, and murdered but most conquering armies. Once they have had their fill, they moved on. But the Romans and Greeks were different. They didn't move on. They stayed and sought to govern, control, and tax. This not only required conquering, plundering soldiers but soldiers that would remain in the communities as law enforcement. This required stable men who were committed to serving in a particular area. Nothing stabilizes a man more than a wife and family. This required breaking the culture of polygamy to make more women available for the soldiers.

It was the first recorded attempt of authorities breaking up monopolies so the little guy could get part of the action. As time went on, laws were made that each man could only have one wife so that the strongest and most effective soldiers would not start building their own harems and, once again, start a shortage of wives, plus the very impractical issue of soldiers having several wives and dozens of children running around the military base.

So now the poor common soldier could have a wife at the base camp even though it was only in a tent, and in these bases raise their families, which they never could have achieved outside of the army. No wonder they signed up in droves. When the army moved the whole camp, the women and children moved with them. This only changed when the European nations developed overseas colonies and empires because it became impossible for the sending country to ship all the families with the soldiers. But for most of the wars and battles fought throughout the continent of Europe up until the twentieth century, the soldier's families tagged along as well.

Now I know that there is a general understanding that Roman soldiers were not allowed to marry. The actual law was that they couldn't have a marriage contract with a wife, and this was in the earlier stages of the empire. However, that didn't stop them from having de facto marriages on the base as history shows that there were many women and children living on Roman bases with the names of wives and children written on centurion's graves and tombs.

Furthermore, while anyone today who is married has a marriage certificate, this type of legal proof of marriage would only have existed with the high-ranking officers who came from well-to-do families. The emperors didn't want their officers tied down with legal contracts. The common soldier would hardly likely to be in this position. Furthermore, even our marriage certificates, registrations, and licenses of today are not legal contracts. They are records of mutual understandings. This policy started to fall apart at about the time of Christ. Claudius in AD 44 allowed soldiers to marry with contracts and around the time of AD 200. Emperor Septimius Severus lifted the ban completely.

But things continued to get better. What do you think the children (especially the young boys) did in the base camp while their fathers and older brothers were over the next hill fighting a battle? They certainly weren't texting their friends on their iPhones, nor were they simply sitting on a hill watching the action. The young boys were involved in carrying supplies, armor, weapons, and caring for the horses.

So what happened while the battle was raging? Would we see the boys of the respective armies sitting down on the ground swapping baseball cards? Not likely. They had access to the spare weapons, and so they would start fighting the other boys. And because the boys (infants) got involved, we eventually came to call them the infantry, the young boys who fought on the ground when probably most of the men were riding horses.

If I am a warlord, I not only have hordes of men signing up to fight for me because I give every man a wife who wants one, but I know that I can now develop, at no cost to me, my own infantry. Simply put, it was primarily the might and strategy of the Greek and Roman armies that changed society from being poly-to mono-. The church was simply swept up along with it.

It should be pointed out, however, that this change in Greek and Roman societies to monogamous marriages had nothing to do with monogamous sexuality, nor was it intended as a lifelong contract on both parties. The soldiers and men were free to have sex with anyone they wanted to as long as it wasn't another man's wife. They were also free to marry and divorce as many times as they wanted to. What the Greek and Romans didn't want was for one man to monopolize large harems and thereby take woman out of the marriage pool. If a soldier has at least one woman at home in the tent, he is far less likely to dessert the army in search of women.

This would probably be a fitting place to look at Paul's statement that deacons should have only one wife and the supposed theory that this created the great sea change. The Greek expression that Paul used was "*mias gunaikao andra*" and can be interpreted several different ways. One is that he should only have one wife, one is that he should give priority to his first wife, and one is that he shouldn't be a womanizer.

Of all the possible means (and there are more), one thing is for sure, and that is, it definitely wouldn't have been the first one (the husband of one wife). Why? Because that was already the law for the whole Roman Empire. Would a church today, looking for a pastor or elder or deacon, make a stipulation that the applicant could only have one wife? Of course not. It would become a huge joke. Why? Because it is already the law that a man could only have one wife.

Therefore, the most reasonable meaning that Paul was alluding to was that he must not be a womanizer. This would be in keeping with the other requirements of not being a drunkard, etc.

Martin Luther said, "I confess that I cannot forbid a person to marry several wives, for it does not contradict the Scripture. If a man wishes to marry more than one wife, he should be asked whether he is satisfied in his conscience that he may do so in accordance with the word of God. In such a case, the civil authority has nothing to do in the matter."

He once advised an inhabitant of Orlamünde to take a second wife in addition to the one then living. Luther also reluctantly approved of a bigamous marriage in the case of Philip, landgrave of Hesse, who was united to a secondary wife, Margarethe von der Saale, on March 4, 1540.

What must be clearly pointed out is what the purpose of having a wife was in ancient times, including the time of Christ. We associate the word wife for someone we love, our sexual partner, and to be a significant part of our lives. The purpose of a wife was, in ancient times, as we have already discussed, was to preserve the family linage. Perhaps the "pedigree brood cow" would be a better expression. Remember, the word "wife" is tied up with the word ownership, not love, commitment, companion, partner, or any other word that we affiliate with the word "wife" today.

This then was the fundamental purpose of marriage in Greek and Roman cultures. In many ways, the marriages of the Greeks and Romans were very similar to what we would call "domestic partnership" contracts of today.

Several years ago, the French government started promoting the program of registered domestic partnership contracts in an endeavor to accommodate the gay community because France does not allow gay marriage. The interesting thing is that not very many gay people took advantage of the program offered, but there was a great response from the heterosexual community because they did not want all the legal entanglements of a traditional divorce if the marriage didn't work out.

Under the program, any two people could register as domestic partners at a government office with all the rights and privileges of a married couple. However, if the relationship didn't work out, only one partner needed to go down to the government office and cancel the contract, and it was then nulled and voided.

There would be none of the ugly fiascos that we often see in a traditional divorce. Apart from the fact that only a man could cancel the contract, this is very much what a marriage was in the times that we are speaking of.

Israel C. S. Lim said the following, "One area of total distortion was that of marital relationship. Surprising to almost all of us, it was common for Catholic priests to have multiple wives and mistresses. In AD 726, it was acceptable for a man with a sick wife to take a second wife so long as he looked after the first one. It was not uncommon among them for a man to have had half a dozen wives with concerns for protecting church property from inheritance; however offspring could not inherit church property, and it was later declared that all sons of priests were illegitimate. In 1022, Pope Benedict VIII banned marriages for priests (monogamous or polygamous). Finally, in 1139, Pope Innocent II voided all marriages of priests, and all new priests had to divorce their wives. All these were done to possess and protect money and church property. Making polygamy a sin and marriage unacceptable for a priest was a slow and purposeful process."

He continued, "Backing up this hidden agenda was a Greek doctrine called asceticism, the paganistic teaching that to be spiritual is to be poor, thus sex and all human passions would have to be denied for the highest fulfillment found only in monastic lifestyle. This distorted view of human passions, and sexuality put a terrible burden on the shoulders of all who wanted to be spiritual. Worse still, it became the root and the source of much more other lies and deception regarding holiness and marriage forms in the whole Christian world.

"Celibacy was propagated as the new standard of high attainment in holiness. Sex was taken to be unclean and sinful. Marriages were painted, at best, as being a necessary evil to guard against sexual sins, such as fornication. Because of such a heathen belief, monks and nuns were considered holier and closer to God than anybody else, and priests would necessarily be celibates. Marriage was considered an activity of the flesh, if possible, to be avoided by those seeking spirituality. Thus monogamy would be tolerated as an acceptable norm among the "less spiritual," and polygamy would be condemned as an abomination. Clearly, Greek philosophy and Roman monogamy were in control of the entire church. This prevailed in what is known as the Dark Ages of the church.

The three hundred years leading up to the conversion of Constantine saw a blend of two cultures. It appears that the church gradually left its polygamous roots and conformed to the pagan culture around it. Just as the Christian church of today has surrendered to the pagan beliefs of secular humanism, so the early church surrendered its historical roots, regarding marriage, to monogamy. However, it would also be fair to say that in that blend, it sought to curb the sexual excesses of the Greek and Roman cultures.

But it would also appear that in this endeavor to curb these sexual excesses that they almost legislated sexuality out of existence. In fact, in a manner of speaking, they did legislate it out of existence, except for the sole purpose of procreation. It is interesting to note that because of, or in spite of, what was happening, the civilized world sank into what we now call the Dark Ages."

Lim continued, "Thus we see how Christianity was corrupted with the Greco-Roman philosophy and values to the point of being almost totally heathen, bowing down to saints and angels, paying for salvation with money and penance. Despite reformations and revivals in the fifteenth century that challenged and overthrew the ritualistic corruption, Greco-Roman values, and interpretation of the Bible are still very much in the Christian lifestyle. This includes enforced monogamy.

Christianity today is still very much Romanized where monogamy is law rather than being Hebraic in nature where polygamy was well accepted in the sight of God and man. By renouncing the Jews, the ways of the patriarchal fathers and their ways were also renounced, thus so was biblical polygamy. This was a big mistake of the early church.

In Germany, after Martin Luther had started the Protestant Reformation, he married a former Catholic nun. And when she was very sick, she suggested to him that he take a second wife.

For political purposes, young Prince Philip of Hesse was arranged to marry the daughter of Duke George. This unhappy union led him to several affairs at a later time, for which he felt so condemned that he refrained from the Lord's Supper. He could have easily annulled his marriage through the Roman Catholic church, which was a common procedure that would not have caused the slightest comment. But being an avowed Lutheran, he refused to consider this way out but instead considered to keep his first wife and marry another woman, a charming seventeen-year-old Margaret von der Saale. After winning the girl's approval, he approached her mother who said, 'We must not break God's laws!' Martin Luther and Melanchthon, a fellow reformer, was consulted. After much consideration with seven other prominent men, a letter was jointly signed with the approval given, but he was told to keep it a secret. Philip lived with his two wives and had children through them. Soon the secret leaked out and the reformation was placed in severe jeopardy because the penalty for bigamy in the Holy Roman Empire was death.

> **Christianity was propagated from the Roman Empire into the West and from the West into the rest of the modern world. And wherever the gospel is preached, Roman monogamy was portrayed as God's only divine standard. Luther could not change it. There was too much to undo. But because the major part of the world is still unchristianized, there are actually many more societies of the world that are polygamous than monogamous.**

A worldwide ethnographic survey of 849 human societies shows 708, whose customs are polygamous (more than 1 wife), 4 polyandrous (more than 1 husband), and 137 monogamous. Other than the religious and supremacy factors, there can be a few other reasons for this."

Lim concluded, "History brings forth conclusive evidence. The enforced should be monogamy, no matter how much it is sanctioned legally or socially or how righteous it is portrayed religiously. It never originated from the Scriptures and has never been set as the only standard for marriage by God. It originated from the pagan Romans that had and are still overtaking the world under the modern title Greco-Roman worldview."

And so we can see that this was a typical example of the church recoiling so far from one excess that it falls backward into another, whereby almost any form of sexuality was sinful. Of course, this also is in part due to the personal experience of Augustine who, as a young man, was extremely sexually permissive and then, after his conversion to Christianity, set out on the warpath against sexuality.

What conclusion can we come to regarding biblical sexuality? In my thinking, we haven't come far from the Jews of old with their Talmud and their endeavor to have every aspect of their lives legally in accordance with what God has dictated for them. The problem is that this is what Christ was supposed to set us free from. Even Jesus said to the religious leaders of His day, "You search the scriptures because you think that in doing so you will have eternal life" (John 5:39). Paul echoed the same sentiment when he said to the early Christians, "You study the scriptures without ever coming to a knowledge of the truth" (2 Timothy 3:7).

When the learned people of Jesus's day tried to nail him down on issues, He didn't respond but told them that the great commandment was to love God with your heart, soul, mind, and strength and your neighbor as yourself. Even then, the rich young ruler didn't get it as he was obviously a conservative evangelical Christian and asked Jesus to tell him who his neighbor was.

It is shameful that so many evangelical Christians live by chapter and verse of the Bible and look to the Bible for an answer on about every issue in life, including sexuality, but are unable to see the forest for the trees.

I once knew a woman, who I will call Linda, who was a good evangelical Christian and had four wonderful Christian daughters. The whole family, including her husband, were very involved in their church.

Unfortunately, Linda had a nervous breakdown and went to stay at some friend's home for a few weeks. While she was gone, one of the girls confided in a church member that they were staying with that their father had been sexually molesting them. The authorities were informed, and the father was imprisoned for twenty years.

Linda was beside herself when she found out and wanted to divorce him but firmly believed that the only biblical grounds for divorce was for adultery. She went to several pastors and Christian counselors, and they all told her the same thing. Fortunately, she finally found a pastor who told her that what the father had done to his daughters was in fact an act of adultery, and therefore, according to the Bible, she was free to divorce him, which she did.

When she told me her story, I was so incensed that Christian leaders could be so out of touch with the fundamental principles of the Bible that they would make her suffer for so long in this emotional torment.

Not one of these knuckleheads had enough sense to study what the Bible really taught about divorce. If they had, they would have known that nowhere in the Bible is there any reference to a woman divorcing her husband, as according to the Talmud it wasn't possible for a woman to divorce her husband. Every reference given about divorce is one given to men because, in biblical times, a man could, for any reason, simply throw his wife out on the street. No man could even take her in. Moses's command regarding divorce was to at least give a woman a certificate of divorce, which would be an act of kindness so that another man could take her in without being accused of stealing the first man's wife.

Jesus was reinforcing this concept when he addressed men and told them that to divorce their wives would be the same as adultery. It was a statement of Jesus against the unjust treatment of women. Men were permitted to have sex with whoever they wanted to as long as it wasn't another man's wife. They could also have as many wives, mistresses, concubines—you name it—so their position in a marriage was light years away from the precarious position of a woman. So even with God's statements against divorce, we need to realize that they were all for one purpose—to protect women.

Furthermore, divorce was not even necessary in biblical times. If a man didn't want anything more to do with one of his wives, he just simply ignored her and didn't have sex with her anymore. This was what David did with his first wife, Michal (1 Samuel 6:23). The key concept was that, although he didn't want anything more to do with her, she was still taken care of by him. This is why divorce was so damning in biblical times because of what it did to women and was not even necessary.

So with Linda's case, the issue is turned completely on its head without one single pastor she talked to, having any idea that the original purpose of the divorce command was to protect women and an attempt to provide for their well-being. And so we rush off to our Bible study groups to study the Bible so we can learn how to live the Christian life. People, wake up.

The central point of Christian teaching is that the Holy Spirit will teach us and lead us in all things (John 14:6). The disciples were terrified at the thought that Jesus was going to leave them. How would they know how to make decisions in life without having Jesus there to ask for advice? It was when they were expressing their fears concerning this that Jesus told them that, after He left them, the Holy Spirit would come and lead and guide them in all truth (John 16:13).

However, that is not the primary question before us. The primary question is rather, "Is it a sin if men and women fall short of this perfect ideal of marriage? The answer of course is a resounding no. No person in their right mind would say yes.

Rabbi Michael Lerner said, "Marriage has traditionally been a holy union sanctified by some spiritual community, and that is what it ought to remain. The government should have nothing to do with it. Instead, the government should create for its own secular and civic purposes a civil union. All legal rights that the state now gives to married couples should be given to civil unions and (should) confer civil union licenses on people whose unions it has sanctioned, while the marriages will henceforth be the province of any religious or spiritual community and only of those communities. The state will not enforce civil agreements made in connection with a spiritual or religious marriages but only those based on civil unions for which it has issued a license. Similarly, the state will have no power over the dissolution of marriages. The communities that sanction these marriages will have sole jurisdiction over the terms of marriage and divorce and cannot use the state to enforce any of these agreements or arrangements."

Historically, in western civilization, the state had nothing to do with marriages. They issued no licenses and kept no records of marriages. Anyone who has done any research on their family tree will realize that, historically, it was the church that decided who could and could not get married, determined what a marriage was, kept all the relevant records, and determined the conditions for divorce. The state had nothing to do with it.

You will remember that in the old wedding ceremony of the Protestant churches there was an opportunity given by the minister for anyone who believed that the couple could not legally be married for some reason, that they were to speak up or forever hold their peace. In other words, speak now or be forever silent. This section of the ceremony has now been dropped in many instances, as it has become redundant due to the fact that the state has taken the responsibility of determining legitimacy for marriage by issuing marriage licenses.

With all the confusion and clouds covering the issue of marriages today, Michael Lerner's approach is not only the only one that makes sense but is in fact going back to how things were done historically in western civilizations.

It is preposterous to think that if an individual files for divorce that the state can determine how long they have to wait until they can remarry. In a free society an individual should be allowed to file for divorce in the morning and get married in the afternoon of the same day if they so choose. It's none of the government's business.

When I was in college many decades ago, a good friend of mine went to a very primitive country in the world as a missionary. He was single when he went but fell in love with a missionary nurse, and they decided to get married. He wrote to me, asking if I could come and be his best man at his wedding.

Of course I was prepared to move heaven and earth to go on this "once in a life time adventure" for two weeks. While I was there,

I spent a great deal of time out with the native people observing and very often being involved with their local cultural activities. I naturally became aware that polygamy was the order of the day and so asked my friend what the position of polygamy was from the perspective of the mission organization who sponsored the mission he was involved with.

He told me that their position was one of telling men who became Christians that they could keep and care for all their wives but could only have sex with their first wife. I didn't say much, but a lot of thoughts went through my mind.

1.  So now that a man has become a Christian, it means that several women, who have been faithful and loving wives, would no longer experience the joy of sex for as long as they lived. How Christian is that?
2.  This would also mean that if these wives had no children, they would never have any children, and of course, in that cultural, a woman having her own children was paramount even to the point of life and death.
3.  Because this was an evangelical conservative mission, it would also mean that none of the wives could divorce their husband in the hope of finding another man.

Wow. And we call this "spreading the good news of Jesus Christ"?

Now let's fast-forward several decades of my life to my involvement in another mission on the other side of the world. While this country was still very primitive, it was also primarily into demon worship.

Once again, the issue of polygamy was a question. However, the mission was not run by missionaries from a western country but by the indigenous pastors and leaders of the native church. The problem was that, with a man having several wives, there was an extreme shortage of Christian women to be wives for the Christian men. The Christian men obviously did not want to marry a woman who was a demon worshipper.

So the indigenous church leaders came up with a voluntary solution. It seems that these native people had a much wider grasp on Paul's statement that "the letter of the law kills, but the spirit of the law gives life" and were not entrenched in blind legalism as were their western brothers and sisters.

They decided to ask the men and wives of polygamous marriages to consider allowing some of the wives to divorce in order to allow them to marry a single Christian man who wanted to get married. There was nothing in the exercise that was arbitrary as it was simply left to individual people and family units to work out what worked best for them.

Their solution was an outstanding success. I was severely tempted to ask the Christian leaders if they would consider sending some of their people, as missionaries, to America to explain Paul's statement to them, which, of course, is at the very heart of all scriptural truth.

In concluding the argument for polygamy, I want to make it perfectly clear that this was not God's original purpose for mankind. It is abundantly clear that God intended for us to have a monogamous relationship by the simple fact that he made one man and one woman, and ever since, all new births have been almost 50 percent of each gender.

The issue is as to whether multiple wives, or husbands, is sinful or wrong, and the answer is a resounding no.

Just as it was never God's intention for us to work for a living or wear clothes or for women to have pain in childbearing, so it wasn't His plan for there to be polygamy. All these things came about because of man's sin. So if we are to say that polygamy is sinful, we would also have to say that wearing clothes, working for a living, and women having pain in childbearing are sinful also. However, there would be nobody that would advocate that any of these were sinful or wrong.

A further consideration was that, in ancient times, men would kill each other in droves. And if polygamy hadn't become the norm, the human race may have very well died out due to there not being enough men to populate the world with only having one wife. Further

still, who was going to care for all these women who had no husbands because there were not enough men to go around? Polygamy
catered to all these needs.

CHAPTER 7

# A Woman's Place

A woman was the gateway through which
God found entrance to humankind.
Women understand not only with the
intellect but also with the heart.
The soul of a woman is fashioned as a shelter
in which other souls may unfold.

**—St. Teresa Benedicta of the Cross
(Carmelite Spiritual Center)**

With the role of women in leadership becoming more visible in today's world, it might be a good time to reevaluate God's intention for the role of women in the church, in society, and the world in general.

The accepted concept is that the Old Testament was a patriarchal society and that this was God's plan. This has been the prevailing attitude for the past two thousand years, and only in recent years has the church and society at large opened up to the concept of sharing leadership roles with women.

However, there still seems to be a significant section of the Christian church that holds to the concept that the patriarchal concept was God's idea.

**The truth is, the patriarchal concept was not God's original idea.**

The fact that a husband would rule over his wife was a result of the fall and one of the three punishments that God gave to Eve for eating the forbidden fruit.

The question is why, apart from the universal punishments, did Adam only get one and Eve get three? The obvious answer would suggest that it was because she sinned first. While that could be the reason, I believe there is more to the story which lies beneath the surface.

With regard to God's intended place for woman, I want to present three arguments that, at first glance, or considered separately, don't seem to be related to each other. However, as we stand back and consider all three perspectives together, we see something really powerful and illuminating.

First, let's back up a little and look at the creation order (Genesis chapter 1).

Day 1: God created light.

Day 2: God created planet earth.

Day 3: God created land and sea and then vegetation.

Day 4: God created the galaxy, the stars, and the sun.

Day 5: God created birds and fish.

Day 6: God created land animals and man. He then put man in the Garden of Eden to care for it, and then finally He created Eve.

Let's pause for a moment and look at the order of God's creation.

It appears that God created something after he had prepared the environment for it with a distinct ascending order. It appears that for each thing that was created, its primary purpose was to serve the next item of creation.

For example, the reason for the need of a planet was so God could create sea, land, and vegetation upon it. The reason he created sea and land vegetation was so that he could put fish in the sea and vegetation on the land for the animals. He then made man because all had been prepared for him: land to live on, fish, vegetation, and animals to eat. He created the Garden of Eden and then put Adam in it. All had been prepared in a logical sequential order for paradise.

Finally, God's crowning masterpiece was His creation of a woman. Eve was the pinnacle of God' creation. God created the Garden of Eden and then created man so he could manage it, and then he created women for her to manage man.

This will come as a shock for most Christians, but we cannot deny the order of God's creation with a definite purpose in the order. I don't think that God intended women to manage men, but what I want to point out is that women had a special place in God's creation order, which I don't think we truly understand or appreciate even to this day.

Marg Mowczko helps us understand some misinterpreted verses.

## *Helper (Ezer) in Genesis 2*

In Genesis 2:18, God is recorded as saying, "It is not good for the (hu)man to be alone. I will make a helper corresponding to him" (cf. Genesis 2:20). The word translated into English as "helper." Here is the Hebrew word *ezer* (pronounced ay-zar).

*Ezer* occurs twenty-one times in the Old Testament. Twice it is used to describe the first woman. Three times it is used of people helping (or failing to help) in life-threatening situations. Sixteen times it is used in reference to God as a helper.

**Without exception, these texts are talking about a vital, urgent, powerful kind of help."**

The concept of women taking a subservient position to men was never part of God's plan or intention. The patriarchal practice came as a result of Eve's disobedience in that her husband would rule over her. In fact, the Hebrew word that is translated, helper, is the same Hebrew word that Jesus used when he said that, when He went back to heaven, He would send the Holy Spirit to be our comforter (John 14:6).

However, that is a very bad translation as we understand the Holy Spirit is the one that empowers us. And so, while it seems difficult to grasp, in essence, God was saying that

**as the Holy Spirit is to the Christian, so
the woman is to be to the man.**

There is also another factor to consider. Why did Satan tempt Eve and not Adam? I believe it is because he was aware that she was either the leader or the person of influence in the equation. He knew, if he had Eve, he also had Adam. This is a significant concept to consider. Since the time of the fall, mankind has sought to go back to the Garden of Eden and have a relationship with God, like Adam and Eve had.

**The question is, why has it taken us six thousand
years to realize that part of having that relationship
with God involves recognizing the rightful place
of women as the pinnacle of God's creation?**

The early church fathers believed that Mary was the counterpart to Eve. If that is true, and I believe it is, then the curse put on Eve, which resulted in the patriarchal system, should have ended with Christ, and women should have been restored to their rightful place as the pinnacle of God's creation.

**The subjugation of God's masterpiece is probably
the greatest example we have of man's depravity.**

The teaching and practice of male patriarchy is nothing more than the sinful perpetuation of the curse put on Eve and was supposed to be lifted with the coming of Christ. If a man believes and practices male patriarchy, he should go and sow weeds in his garden or fields so that he can pull them out with the sweat of his brow when they grow up. Failure to do so would be nothing more than blatant hypocrisy.

Chesna Hinkley said the following, "Many Christians believe that strict gender roles—men lead, and women submit—are God-ordained. They attempt to find support for this claim in Genesis, pointing to 'creation order.' Some argue that because God made Adam before Eve, Adam occupies a special position and wields authority over her. Historically, many have suggested that Eve's creation from a 'rib' makes her Adam's inferior. You may hear the term 'helpmate' to describe Eve's supposedly submissive orientation toward Adam. Some in Christian history have extrapolated from creation order that women do not bear the image of God. It's rare today to claim this belief outright, but it persists in the idea that Eve was created for Adam and, therefore, that all women exist for the purposes of men.

But when we look at the creation stories in Genesis, we see an emphasis not on Adam and Eve's difference but on their sameness ('bone of my bone and flesh of my flesh'). Though Eve (and women with her) has been reduced to a servant in need of constant male guidance, the Hebrew indicates that she's the only being in God's creation that could match Adam as an equal. Eve is not Adam's inferior, she's his perfect partner.

What about the rib? The word *tsela*, which has been mistranslated 'rib' for many centuries, really means 'side' or 'leaf.' This is the only time in the Old Testament that it's translated 'rib,' and this is because of speculation and tales from the ancient rabbis.

Picture a pair of swinging saloon doors. Each swinging panel is a *tsela*. As we'll see below, the term 'helpmeet' suggests the same: Man and woman are two sides of one thing. They're mirror images, if you will, and both are necessary to make up the whole. God took enough of the original human to make another creature (Eve) that was like him. In the New Testament, this is important for understanding the Pauline concept of 'headship.' Eve was created out of Adam so that they can be the same: equally made in the image of God, identical in purpose (ruling the earth), and mutual in relationship.

Doesn't Adam have authority because he came first?

The episode with the animals is meant to show us that nothing below the man will be 'meet' for him. If the man had authority over the woman because he came first, the animals would have authority over the man. Instead, the man and the woman are the crowning piece of creation, coming at the end.

**In fact, 1 Corinthians chapter 11 may imply that
Eve has an even greater glory, being the last piece of
creation and the one who completes humanity.**

The creation of Eve shows us that contrary to what patriarchal culture would have us believe, women are a crucial part of the whole human endeavor—not just filling the earth but ruling it too (Genesis 1:28)."

Dr. Kenneth Howel was a Presbyterian minister who switched to Catholicism and said the following in regard to Mary being the New Eve, "The concept of the New Eve taught by the Church Fathers is a summary and natural extension of Paul's doctrine of Christ as the New Adam. Irenaeus based his teaching on Ephesians 1:10 where Paul says that God sent Christ as a plan [*oikonomia*] for the fullness of time, to unite all things in him, things in heaven, and things on earth. For Paul and Irenaeus, God arranged salvation history in such a way that all reality would be incarnated in His Son, Jesus Christ. Everything was put under Christ's headship (thus recapitulate). This divine arrangement not only that Christ, by His obedience, reversed the effects of Adam's sin but also that Mary, by her obedience, reversed the effects of Eve's rebellion.

The only difference is that Mary's obedience was derived from her Son's obedience. She was made a part of his saving plan because Christ made her 'full of grace' (Luke 1:28). The phrase 'New Eve' or similar expressions occur in the early Church Fathers. Take, for example, Justin Martyr, who wrote within a couple of generations of the apostles. In his *Dialogue with Trypho the Jew* (ca. AD 150), Justin explains that Christ destroyed Satan's work in the same way evil originally entered the world. Evil entered through Eve while she was still a virgin, so too salvation entered through Mary while she was still a virgin. Each woman willingly participated in the act they performed. Neither was an unconscious instrument. Eve listened to the serpent and conceived death. Irenaeus says that Eve, 'by disobeying became the cause of death for herself and the whole human race, so also Mary was obedient and became the cause of salvation for herself and the whole human race' (*Against Heresies* 3.22.4).

Later he said of these two virgins, "Just as the human race was subject to death by a virgin, it was freed by a virgin, with the virginal disobedience balanced by virginal obedience."

In an article of *God's Word to Women*, we have the following: "Usages of *ezer* in the Old Testament show that, in most cases, God is an *ezer* to human beings, which calls to question if the word 'helper' is a valid interpretation. The article below by William Sulik explains this point quite well. He references R. David Freedman.

"The noun *ezer* occurs twenty-one times in the Old Testament. In many of the passages, it is used in parallelism to words that clearly denote strength or power.

Therefore, could we conclude that Genesis 2:18 be translated as "I will make a power [or strength] corresponding to man." Freedman even suggested on the basis of later Hebrew that the second word in the Hebrew expression found in this verse should be rendered equal to him. If so, then God makes for the man a woman fully his equal and fully his match. In this way, the man's loneliness will be assuaged.

The same line of reasoning occurs with the apostle Paul who urged in 1 Corinthians 11:10, "For this reason, a woman must have power [or authority] on her head [that is to say, invested in her]."

This line of reasoning, which stresses full equality, is continued in Genesis 2:23 where Adam said of Eve, "This is now bone of my bones and flesh of my flesh; she shall be called 'woman,' for she was taken out of man." The idiomatic sense of this phrase "bone of my bones" is a "very close relative" to "one of us" or in effect "our equal."

The woman was never meant to be an assistant or helpmate to the man. The word "mate" slipped into English since it was so close to the Old English word "meet," which means "fit to" or "corresponding to" the man, which comes from the phrase that likely means "equal to." What God had intended then was to make a "power" or "strength" for the man who would, in every way, "correspond to him" or even "be his equal." The Torah study for Reform Jews says, from the time of creation, relationships between spouses have at times been adversarial. In Genesis 2:18, God calls woman an *ezer kenegdo*, a "helper against him." The great commentator Rashi took the term literally to make a wonderful point: "if he [Adam] is worthy [she will be a helper—*ezer*]. If he is not worthy [she will be] against him [*kenegdo*] for strife." This Jewish study also described man and woman facing each other with arms raised, holding an arch between them, giving a beautiful picture of equal responsibility."

Many have misunderstood the reference that Paul made in Ephesians 5:3 and Colossians 1:18 regarding the man being the head of the woman.

Again, Mowczko addressed this issue, "In Colossians 1:18, Paul writes, '[The Son] is the head (*kephalē*) of the church body of which he is the beginning (*archē*), the firstborn of the dead, so that he himself may be first in everything.'

Paul's main point in the passage where this verse comes from (Colossians 1:15–18) is to show that Jesus is the creator, origin, and beginning of everything in the universe. This includes Jesus being the 'author' of the church. Paul used the word *kephalē* (head) in this context—the context of origin and beginning or, as some say, 'source.'

"In English, the word 'head' has many meanings. One metaphorical meaning of head is 'leader' or 'chief person.' In English, the 'head' of an organization is the leader, the top person. In Koine Greek, the language of the New Testament, the word *kephalē* (head) also has metaphorical meanings. However, 'leader' or 'chief person' is usually not one of them. Unfortunately, many Christians have simply presumed that 'head' refers to authority in 1 Corinthians 11:3 and Ephesians 5:23, and many churches continue to teach this interpretation."

Even today, in our English language, we use the expression "head" as a reference to "source" with such expressions as the origins of a stream or river being the "headwaters" or the origin of the water. So to paraphrase, Paul was saying that Christ is the source of man, and man is the source of woman, and God is the source of Christ (1 Corinthians 11:13).

The second point for us to consider is that of matriarchal societies.

There has never been a society or group of people found where the matriarchal society is the simple reverse of the patriarchal society. What we do have, however, are societies that are called matriarchal but with different roles for each gender to play. Most of these groups are found among the North American indigenous people and also the indigenous natives of some of the Pacific Islands and of Australia. The characteristic of these matriarchal societies is that the women play the primary role. Only a woman can own land, all children born belong to the mother's clan or family and have the clan's name. The women make all the decisions as to what happens in the village. Sometimes the chief is a man, but he is elected by the women and can be removed by the women any time they choose.

The men have four primary functions:

a)  To hunt for food, although the women will tell the men what food they want.
b)  To go to war to protect the village, but the women will tell the men who and when to fight.
c)  To father children.
d)  To teach manhood to their sisters, sons, or their nephews.

However, there are two characteristics that are present in all matriarchal societies. One is peacefulness, and the other is that none of them had influence or contact with Christian Europe until a few hundred years ago.

Joseph Nye is a former US Assistant Secretary of Defense and is a professor at Harvard and the author of *The Future of Power*. He asked the question, "Would the world be more peaceful if women were in charge?" A challenging new book by the Harvard University psychologist Steven Pinker said that the answer is "yes."

In *The Better Angels of Our Nature*, Pinker presented data, showing that human violence, while still very much with us today, has been gradually declining. Moreover, he said, "Over the long sweep of history, women have been and will be a pacifying force.

**Traditional war is a man's game: tribal women never band together to raid neighboring villages.**

As mothers, women have evolutionary incentives to maintain peaceful conditions in which to nurture their offspring and ensure that their genes survive into the next generation. Women's nonhierarchical style and relational skills fit a leadership need in the new world of knowledge-based organizations and groups that men, on average, are less well prepared to meet.

Now, however, with the information revolution and democratization demanding more participatory leadership, the 'feminine style' is becoming a path to more effective leadership. In order to lead successfully, men will not only have to value this style in their women colleagues but will also have to master the same skills. This bias is beginning to break down in information-based societies, but it is a mistake to identify the new type of leadership we need in an information age simply as 'a woman's world.'

"Even positive stereotypes are bad for women, men, and effective leadership. The key choices about war and peace in our future will depend not on gender but on how leaders combine hard-and soft-power skills to produce smart strategies. Both men and women will make those decisions. But Pinker is probably correct when he notes that the parts of the world that lag in the decline of violence are also the parts that lag in the empowerment of women."

The third point that we need to look at is how women have fared as leaders of nations. Let's take modern history or the last two hundred years. Although there have been many capable and successful women in national leadership, it may be pertinent to point out that never has a country with a woman as leader attacked another country. There have been three incidents where countries with a man, as the leader, have tried to invade a country where a woman was the leader. In all three incidents, the country with the woman leader successfully prevented an invasion and defended her country. However, the woman leader not only defended her country to the original border but did not use her country's superior military strength to invade the belligerent power and take land from them.

History will show that, usually when the country that has a man as a leader has to defend against a belligerent nation, he will not only defend his country but will use it as an excuse to totally invade and annex the belligerent country or portions of it. This occupation of the now new invading country festers for years, decades, and centuries, but inevitability resentment boils over, resulting in more war and bloodshed.

The three countries that I am referring to are the British defenses against the Argentinian invaders of the British-owned Falkland Islands by Prime Minister Margaret Thatcher, Israel's successful defense against the invading Syrians under Prime Minister Mrs. Golda, and India's successful defense against the invasion of Pakistan under Prime Minister Mrs. Gandhi.

James Carmichael, in his book, *Israeli Special Forces and Intelligence Services*, makes the following pertinent comment, "There can be few intelligence agencies in the world that carry with them more of a reputation than Mossad or The Institute for [Israeli] Intelligence and Special Operations.

"Some of Mossad's best agents are women. They may lack some of the physicality of their male counterparts, but they bring with them an ability to assess and predict danger that is often missing in men who have always been able to rely on their strength rather than needing to assess danger intuitively."

The fourth and final point is one of observation of the animal kingdom. This example standing by itself does not say much with regard to the role of women. But when taken with the two previous points, I think it adds a powerful voice to my hypotheses. I am no biologist, but it seems to me that in the natural world of animals— and by this, I mean mammals, fish, birds and insects—that rape is virtually impossible. About the only animal that I know of that is capable of rape is the monkey, which also happens to be the closest of the animal species related to humans. With humans, a man is able to rape a woman because of his dexterity and physical superiority of strength.

However, in the animal kingdom if a female does not want to copulate with a male, she only has to lie down, and there is absolutely nothing the male can do about it. Now physically, he could possibly kill her, but I know of no documented evidence where the male of a species killed a female because she did not want to copulate.

In the bird kingdom, the male may be able to get on the female's back, but there are three things that she has to do to make copulation possible. Firstly, she needs to stand still. Secondly, she needs to spread her wings to give him more room to stand on, and then finally, she needs to move her tail to one side so he can squirt his seminal fluid from his vent into her vent. If any one of these three things don't happen, copulation will not happen.

Typically, the female just keeps running from him until he gets tired and tries to find another female. Some have said that ducks are capable of rape, but that is not so. How do I know? Because I raised ducks as a kid. Yes, the drake will often get on her back, but there is absolutely nothing that he can do to force her to move her tail to one side, and therefore copulation just does not happen. The proof of this is that the drake will continually try to copulate with her even after he slides off her back several times because he knows that he hasn't done the deed. So he just keeps trying until he is exhausted, or a kid like me comes along and throws stones at him to make him leave her alone.

With fish, most of them breed by the female laying eggs and then the male spraying them with his sperm. Now it doesn't matter how eager Mr. Fish is to spray his sperm, there is nothing he can do to force her to lay her eggs. His only option is to hurry up and wait. Mrs. Fish is in the driver's seat—end of story.

As we look at the animal kingdom, we will all be aware that if the female and male appear to look different from each other, it is always the male that is the most attractive. For example, who wants to look at a lioness when they can look at the majestic grandeur of the male lion?

In the bird world the difference is even more striking. Yes, there are some birds where the male and female look identical. But we are all aware of the birds where the male has such an array of beautiful colors and markings, while the female looks simply drab. Typically, the male puffs himself up to look attractive if he is of a breed that is capable of this and then sends out a loud signal that he is open for business. Some male birds even prepare a nest for the female to see when she shows up. If a female does show up, the ball is in her court, and she will only mate with him if she does the three things that were mentioned above, and that will only happen if she likes what she sees.

It appears that it is only in the human species, which have been typically patriarchal, that we believe it is the man's role to make the first move and then ultimately propose marriage.

I believe that what happens in the animal kingdom is God's way of showing us that, just as it is in the natural world, the female is the one who will determine who will be the father of her offspring, that this same premise must also hold true with humans.

This is further supported by women's response to rape. While rape, for a male or female, is a traumatic and devastating experience, I think that we can all agree that rape for a woman does something that almost seems irreparable to her physic and inner self. I am no psychologist and don't pretend to be, but I would suggest that this incredible devastation of rape for a woman, at its innermost core, is the revulsion that the right that God gave to her, and to her alone, to decide who would be the father of her baby was brutishly torn from her and was a violation of the very essence of her womanhood and self being.

Tracey. R. Rich shares the following, "Sex should only be experienced in a time of joy. Sex for selfish, personal satisfaction, without regard for the partner's pleasure, is wrong and evil. A man may never force his wife to have sex. A couple may not have sexual relations while drunk or quarreling. Sex may never be used as a weapon against a spouse, either by depriving the spouse of sex or by compelling it. It is a serious offense to use sex (or lack thereof) to punish or manipulate a spouse.

**Sex is the woman's right, not the man's. A man has a duty to give his wife sex regularly and to ensure that sex is pleasurable for her.**

He is also obligated to watch for signs that his wife wants sex and to offer it to her without her asking for it. The woman's right to sexual intercourse is referred to as *onah*, and it is one of a wife's three basic rights (the others are food and clothing), which a husband may not reduce. The Talmud specifies both the quantity and quality of sex that a man must give his wife. It specifies the frequency of sexual obligation based on the husband's occupation, although this obligation can be modified in the ketubah (marriage contract). A man may not take a vow to abstain from sex for an extended period of time and may not take a journey for an extended period of time because that would deprive his wife of sexual relations. In addition, a husband's consistent refusal to engage in sexual relations is grounds for compelling a man to divorce his wife, even if the couple has already fulfilled the halachic obligation to procreate.

Although sex is the woman's right, she does not have absolute discretion to withhold it from her husband. A woman may not withhold sex from her husband as a form of punishment; and if she does, the husband may divorce her without paying the substantial divorce settlement provided for in the ketubah."

The further piece of evidence I would mention that would support God's intention for us to live in a matriarchal society is once again drawn from the animal kingdom. Most of the herd-type animal (let's call them family type) are matriarchal. This would include horses, cattle, goats, lions, elephants, wolves, honeybees, ants, bonobos, meerkats, orcas, etc. to name just a few. Next time you see a group of wild horses galloping across the landscape, take special notice that the stallion is always bringing up the rear. The matriarchal mare is the leader, and she decides where the herd is going to go.

Lesley Evans Ogden said, "What the animals tell us about female leadership, is that there are over 5,000 known species of just mammals that are led by females.

One take-home message that can be drawn from analyzing female leadership in mammals is the crucial importance of coalitions: who you're friends with in your social networks and the expertise that comes with age and experience. Female leadership, the animal world suggests, is more likely to emerge when females form cooperative units."

According to *Mammal Species of the World* by Wilson and Reeder, the most recent authoritative published checklist of modern mammal species, there are 5,416 different species of mammals. This means that in respect to mammals, approximately 95 percent of the species are matriarchal."

This does not even take into consideration the matriarchal societies within the bird and fish world. This is a powerful indication of what God had in mind when he created us and that He intended the human race to be matriarchal also.

## Patriarchy is simply a result of the fall of mankind and is a product of sin.

I can hear a response that would go something like this, "Yes, but we are not animals, as we are created with a moral consciousness in the image of God."

I would respond with an absolute agreement and point out that when it comes to sex, in humans, God made an adjustment to the natural order somewhat. As far as I am aware, there is no creature in the animal kingdom where God created females to want sex other than when she was ovulating. So this would appear that in the animal kingdom, sex was designed by God exclusively for procreation.

However, when we come to the apex of God's creation, we find something quite different. We find that women have a certain part of their anatomy that is designed only for pleasure. God was so particular about this part of a women's anatomy that He created it with over eight thousand nerve endings that, if stimulated, would give her the ultimate—wait for it—climax.

Now I can hear some women saying, "And, yes, with over eight thousand nerve endings, my man can't even find one."

However, this anomaly doesn't stop there. This area of pleasure is in no way tied to her monthly ovulation, which makes it possible for her to get pregnant. For this, the body is designed very much like the animal kingdom in that ovulation happens only a few days each month. Furthermore, the clitoris is available for pleasure and action 24-7, just like a man is wired.

**This therefore is conclusive evidence that sexual pleasure for humanity was an extremely high priority for God in His creation of mankind.**

Finally, when we realize that it was God's original intention that women should take a leadership role in the family and society in general, a lot of other pieces start to fall into place. For example, let's take the issue of the man being the spiritual leader in the home. This is a doctrine that the fundamental evangelicals have been propagating for decades and is the sole reason for the organization of Promise Keepers. However, in life, that paradigm just doesn't work out.

I will use a few examples:

Ask yourself, and maybe even ask others as well, who the person was that had the earliest spiritual impact on you with regard to God and the Christian life. I will guarantee that for the vast majority of people that individual was a woman, probably a mother or grandmother, but it was a woman. I cannot remember how many famous men that I have read of who credit their mother with having a powerful influence on their lives when they were young and especially as it relates to spirituality.

In all of my years as a pastor, I had more women in my congregation coming to church, making an inedible contribution in ministry and service, and whose husbands only came at Christmas and made no profession of faith at all than I could ever count or remember. And yet I could count on one hand, and still not use all my fingers, the number of men I had in my churches who were in the reverse situation.

One of the things that was always a source of encouragement to me, when I was a pastor, was the fact that after Jesus had poured out his life for us, there were only four people with him at the cross—three women and one teenage boy. Nothing much has changed in the last two thousand years. Next time you happen to be involved or attend a meeting in the community for residence who want to improve the social condition of society, take a head count, and you will realize that the same ratio of women to men that Jesus had at the cross is still the same today. It's still roughly a three-to-one ratio.

Ask anyone you know who has served for any amount of time as a missionary in a non-Christian culture, "Who are more open to the gospel, men or women?" and you will get the same answer from whoever you ask, it's women.

So bearing all this in mind, is it not rather preposterous to propagate a doctrine that the man is the spiritual leader in the home when the preponderance of evidence is against such a concept? I'm sure any man reading this will find my observations enlightening and will feel relieved that this burden has been lifted from his shoulders.

**It is still true that "the hand that rocks
the cradle rules the world."
It has been well said that "a man's home is his castle."
And while that may be true, someone forgot to
add that "a woman's home is her kingdom."**

If you have trouble with the above statement, then you need to go talk with a real estate salesperson. All real estate salespeople know that when you are trying to sell a house, the pitch must be made to the woman. The man is usually interested in about four things. Is the garage big enough for my boat and toys? Is the lawn small enough that I can mow it between beers? Is there a place for a couch so I can watch the game? And can we afford it?

While that may seem a bit simplistic, most of you reading this will know that there is a lot of truth to what I have just said. Occasionally, my wife has to be gone for a few days to spend some time with her family. From the time she leaves until the time she comes back, my home makes a dramatic, instant, and inexplicable transformation from a home to just a house—simply four walls and a roof so I can get in out of rain. The moment she steps through the front door, my box becomes a beautiful, warm, and loving home again.

When children can't find an item, who do they ask if they know where it is? Why, of course they ask their father because he is lord and master of the manor. Of course not. You know who they ask—the matriarchal woman of the house. When we men hunt for three days looking for an item because we can't confess to our inadequacies in having to ask her where an item is, we finally surrender and ask the question. She doesn't just say, "It's on the dresser or fridge or in the closet." No, she says, "It's behind your dresser on top of your ammunition, next to some old magazines by some old fishing gear, and along with three single socks that need washing."

There is nothing that can possibly be hidden from the woman of the house. She knows you got up at some time during the night and had ice cream, cookies, and milk. God only knows how, but she knows. And she knows because her home is her kingdom. If you don't believe me, just try messing it up.

I have great respect for the North American native people and the great wisdom that flows from their culture. I recently came across some beautiful and powerful statements.

> **A woman's highest calling is to lead a man to his soul so as to unite him with Source. A man's highest calling is to protect woman, so she is free to walk the earth unharmed. (Cherokee Proverb)**

> **It is the mothers, not the warriors, who create a people and guide their destiny. (Luther Standing Bear Oglala Lakota)**

> **Our women have been chosen by the Creator to be the portal between the spiritual realm and the physical realm, the only force on earth powerful enough to navigate unborn spirits onto this planet. (Tribe unknown)**

# CHAPTER 8

# WOMEN IN THE BIBLE

When we, as Westerners, read the Bible, there is an incredible amount of spiritual truth that we miss purely because of our Western thinking. As Westerners, we mostly think in a lineal pattern or in a logical sequence of thought. Of course, we owe this to the Greeks. However, the people of the Middle East do not think in a lineal manner primarily and mostly communicate with imagery. Judaism is not Western. It is Middle Eastern, and therefore, Christianity is Middle Eastern in its orientation and therefore communicates with regard to metaphysical thought, which would include religion, primarily via spoken imagery. We see this very clearly in the parables of Jesus; but because we think like the Greeks, we only see what Greeks would see.

Take for example the parables of Jesus. When we read them, we do so as individual parables. Have you ever heard a pastor preach a sermon series on the parables? If you have, you know that he or she probably took one particular parable for each sermon without ever realizing how they relate to each other.

So many of our sermons, teaching, and personal Bible studies zero in on what the particular shade of meaning was in Hebrew or Greek, with a magnifying glass. While that type of studying certainly has its place and is necessary, so few people zoom out and look for patterns in the Bible. Just as we can only see some patterns on the ground from the air that we could be walking right over on the ground and never notice, so we do the same with the Bible. The Bible is full of imagery and patterns. I will give you one example and then get back to talking about women.

Most Christians are aware of the seven letters to the seven churches in the book of the Revelation. However, did you realize that John was laying out before us the seven ages of the Christian church? Just so you know, we are in the age of the church at Laodicea the last age that made God want to throw up because it was wealthy yet was not hot nor cold but simply warm. Does that mean that these are not letters to seven churches? No, it means that John had two purposes. One was the letter to the seven different churches, but it was done in such an order that he was telling us in code what the seven ages of the church would be. How do we know this? Because he said at the beginning of chapter 4, "After this I was taken" (Revelation 4:1). If he was simply writing seven letters to seven churches, why would the statement, "after this," be made? That statement tells us that everything that was going to happen in the end-time would happen after the completion of the seven ages.

With regard to how God views women, or more importantly for our purposes of women and sex, we need to zoom out from the details of the Bible. And if we do, we see a pattern of how God considers women when it comes to sexuality.

Let's look at six different women in the Bible who all broke the sexual rules that the evangelical church claims we must live by and see what God's reaction to them was individually.

## Tamar

In Genesis chapter 28, we have a fascinating story. It's the story of Judah, the ancestor of both King David and Christ. Judah had three sons Er, Onan, and Shelah. There is no record of either Er or Onan having any children. The Bible says that Er was wicked and that God killed him. Under the law, if a man died, his brother had to go and have sex with the widow (sister-in-law) called Tamar so that she would have children. As we have already observed, Onan pulled himself out at the appropriate time so that she would not conceive, and God killed him also. This left the youngest son Shelah, who was obviously only a boy. Judah said to Tamar, "Go and live with your family for a few years until Shelah is old enough for you to be his wife."

So Tamar went to live with her family. As time went on, young Shelah grew to be a young man, but Judah, for whatever reason, didn't tell Tamar that it was time for her to go and have sex with him. Of course she realized it was only a matter of time before she would be too old, and Shelah wouldn't want to have sex with her or that she would be past childbearing age. So time was of the essence.

So she devised a plan. She found out that Judah, her father-in-law, was going to be coming to where all the sheepshearing was going to take place and so went and sat by the side of the road that he would be traveling on. She disguised herself and dressed like a prostitute. Sure enough, Judah came along and pulled her to the side of the road to have sex with her. She said, "So how much are you going to pay me?"

He responded, "I'll give you a kid goat from the flock."

Her response was, "How will I know that you will keep your word?"

He asked her, "What do you want me to do to show that I am pledging to you that I will honor my promise?"

She said, "Give me your ring, your staff, and your belt."

So he did so.

When he had finished his shearing, he sent a servant with a kid goat to give to her, but she had vanished. The servant asked around, but she could not be found. So he returned to Judah to tell him that the girl had vanished. Judah's response was very cavalier, and he said, "Well she can keep them. But let's get out of here before we become the laughingstock of the whole village."

A few months later, word got to Judah that Tamar was pregnant and had gotten pregnant through being a prostitute. Judah was pretty incensed ordered that she be brought to him and be burned to death. (You see the reason for his anger was that she was his property. And if she had become pregnant through another man, the father would claim the child.) That would be like having very bad day on the stock market. So she came to Judah and showed him the three items that he had given her in lieu of the goat and said, "It's pretty much a no-brainer. How do you think I got this stuff?" Judah must have been blown out of the saddle and set her free, saying that she was more righteous than he was because he had broken his word in not letting his son, Shelah, have sex with her.

So what happened? She had twin boys. That would be like winning the Super Lottery and not have to pay any tax on it.

So now let's look at the spiritual connotation in this one chapter.

1.  God killed Er because he was wicked, but we have no idea what he did wrong.
2.  God killed his brother Onan because he had sex with his sister-in-law, as was commanded, but he stopped her getting pregnant.
3.  With God striking these two guys dead, I would be pretty leery about doing anything untoward if I was Judah or Tamar.
4.  However, we see Tamar offering herself to Judah as a prostitute. God didn't do anything.
5.  A man having sex with his daughter-in-law was forbidden by the law. By Judah's response in hearing that Tamar had been a prostitute obviously means that prostitution was not allowed either.

We have three violations of sexual behavior by these two people, and God not only does not punish them but blesses them both. Yes, Judah was the proud father of twin boys.

But that's not the end. The second-born son was called Zerah, and one of his descendants was on the cabinet with Nehemiah while rebuilding the wall of Jerusalem. (Nehemiah 11:24) The firstborn son was called Perez, and he got to be not only an ancestor of King David but also of Christ.

This can only lead us to one conclusion, either we have a very strange God, or we have a very strange interpretation of God.

Personally, I'm going to go with the second option as Paul told us in Romans 3:4 that God cannot be wrong. I grew up in the evangelical church and have spent most of my life as pastor, missions director, and evangelist, and I have never once heard any sermon or read any book or article on the above story. Why? Because it flies in the face of contemporary thought, teaching, and dogma on evangelical Christian sexuality. However, these same people believe and maintain that the whole Bible was inspired by God and yet treat this chapter like it doesn't exist.

### So who do you think is correct, God or the contemporary evangelical Christian teaching on biblical sexuality?

I can hear someone saying, "Yes, but that is the Old Testament." To which I would respond, "So on that basis, do you think it is okay to throw out the Ten Commandments?" Nothing changed in what God thought to be right or wrong between the two testaments, as He has said, "I the Lord your God do not change" (Malachi 3:6).

Only two things changed in the New Testament: (1) Christ opened the way for us to have direct access to God, and (2) the Holy Spirit was sent to enable us to be lead of the Spirit and empowered by the Spirit so that God could use our lives as a living sacrifice in order to accomplish His purposes.

However, there is another principle here to be looked at. I had an old professor in college who once said, "When two godly principles clash, we are to take the road of the higher love."

So here we have the clash of two principles. On the one hand, prostitution was not sanctioned, and sex between a man and his daughter-in-law was strictly prohibited. Yet on the other hand, a woman with no sons to care for her and protect her in her old age was something God wanted no woman to experience. So as far as God was concerned, care for Tamar was an expression of a greater love, which canceled out the sexual prohibitions.

We have this story preserved down through the ages to show us that sexual discipline, while being part of Christian discipline, must not stand in the way of making it possible for a widow woman to have a son, along with all the advantages that having a son would mean. To put it simply, it seems that, according to God's economy, "The end sometimes justifies the means." And yet beyond that, it shows us the incredible love and compassion that God has toward women.

## Rahab

The story of Rahab is found in the book of Joshua. Joshua sent two spies into Canaan to check the defensive positions of Jericho. It appears that they must have disguised themselves very well because they were able to enter the city undetected and spent the night with Rahab the prostitute. Rahab told them that inhabitants of the city were terrified and that she basically wanted to become one of the Israelites and worship their God.

We know the rest of the story whereby she was the only inhabitant in the city that God spared because of her decision. Once again, we have a strange situation whereby a prostitute is not only the only one spared, but she becomes an ancestor of Christ.

## Bathsheba

The story of Bethsheba is found in 2 Samuel chapter 11. She was the daughter of one of King David's main military and governmental officers named Eliam (2 Samuel 11:3) and was one of David's closest friends. David had probably known her all of her life. She married an army officer called Uriah who would have had a very high status due to the fact that Bathsheba lived right next door to the palace. Only the elite among the elite lived in such areas. David and Bathsheba would have been good friends, and slowly, an infatuation started that ended in a full-blown adulterous affair.

David would have first seen Bathsheba when she was a baby, and probably, as she grew up, David became her hero. David planned carefully and sent his army off on a military action and did something that he had never done before. He allowed Joab, his five-star general or field marshal, to lead the army while he stayed home. David made this first move in deploying his army and all the men from around the palace.

There is no record of him ever doing anything like this before. However, Bathsheba made the second move and decided to do a very inappropriate thing by going out onto the back deck of her home, knowing that the palace balcony overlooked her deck, to do her "ceremonial washing," which would have included her removing most of her clothing. That was distinct and purposeful ploy on her part. David then sent for her, and they had sex, and she became pregnant. What throws the reader a curveball is that he asked a servant to go and get her to find out who she was. This was supposed to throw the servant and any others listening off the scent. How naive can you get? They all knew what was going on. It was a complete set up. David then arranged for Bathsheba's husband, Uriah, to come and report to him on the battle; and after the report, David told him go home for the night to be with his wife. It is obvious from Uriah's behavior that he knew all about the infatuation that had been brewing between his wife and David because he refused to go.

David was getting desperate to cover his tracks and said that he could stay at the palace and thereby proceeded to get him drunk in the hope that he would go home before he went back to the battlefront. However, Uriah still refused to go home and spent the night outside the palace gates so everyone could see that he never went home to be with his wife. He obviously knew what David was trying to do. David then sent him back to the battle with sealed instructions to be given to Joab that he was to place Uriah in a position where he would be killed. Joab obeyed the command, and he was killed, and David was then able to marry Bathsheba before the baby was born.

Nathan the prophet confronted David with his sin whereby he truly repented, but the damage was done. The baby died when it was a few weeks old. The repercussions for David were horrendous. While God forgave him, I don't think he ever forgave himself. His kingdom began to deteriorate from that day forward, and he was never the same man again.

God not only forgave them both but evidenced his great mercy by allowing David and Bathsheba to give birth to another son, who was Solomon, and a direct ancestor of Christ. This picture is such a beautiful one in portraying the total forgiveness of God, just like it didn't happen. But here is the point. Nowhere in the Bible do we find any reference of Bathsheba doing anything wrong. She clearly had a part in the set up and knew exactly what she was doing, and yet there is no condemnation of her anywhere in scripture.

## Ruth

The story of Ruth is an interesting one also. She was a godly woman who needed an Israelite husband. Without going into all the details of the story, as you can read them in the book of Ruth, her most likely chance was a wealthy relative of hers named Boaz. But how to get Boaz's attention was the problem. She played a few games in the field to flirt with him as instructed by her mother-in-law, Naomi, but that didn't seem to produce the desired results.

Her mother-in-law, Naomi, told her to go to his bed after the party at the close of the harvest and climb into his bed to have sex with him. Oh yes we all know that the Bible says, "She 'uncovered his feet and lay at his feet,' but that was just a euphemism for uncovering his genitals. Just like when we say a couple slept with each other, we know that not much sleeping took place, for what we really mean is that the couple had sex. That was what "uncovering his feet" and "'lying at his feet" meant. Nowhere in the Bible is there any sugges-tion that Naomi or Ruth did anything sinful or wrong.

## Lot's daughters

In Genesis 19:30–38, we have another poignant story.

Abraham's nephew Lot had chosen to live in one of the cities of Sodom and Gomorrah, which was about to be destroyed by God. However, Abraham plead with God to spare Lot and his family, so God sent an angel to lead Lot, his wife, and his two daughters out of the city and to safety in the mountains. He ended up not running to the mountains but to a small town nearby called Zoar and took ref-uge there. Lot's wife looked back at the cities being destroyed and was turned into a pillar of salt. After a short time in Zoar, they fled to the mountains and took refuge in a cave. After all, the dust had settled, and they had settled into living in a cave, the daughters realized, that were up the proverbial creek without a paddle.

They said to each other, "There are no men around here to have sex with, and so we are doomed." Notice they didn't say, "There are no men around here for us to marry." They obviously didn't equate the fact that marriage was a prerequisite for sex.

They decided to get their father drunk and to go and have sex with him. The older daughter did it first. And when she told her younger sister that she was pregnant, the younger sister did the same thing and became pregnant also. They both had sons.

There is absolutely no suggestion in the Bible anywhere that they had done anything wrong.

## The woman taken in adultery

In the Gospel of John chapter 8, we have the story of the woman taken in adultery. Under the Mosaic law, if a woman was found guilty of adultery, she was to be stoned. It was perfectly acceptable for men to commit adultery because, according to their logic, they weren't guilty. It was the woman who was guilty for tempting them to have sex with her. Now it must be remembered that if a woman would risk the terrible and barbaric death of stoning that she must have been living such a horrendous life of suffering and abuse that she was prepared to suffer the fate of death by stoning rather than continue in her horrific dilemma.

The Pharisees thought that they had Jesus in a corner that He couldn't get out of. They asked him what they should do and reminded Him that according to the law of Moses, she must be stoned. We all know the story well. Jesus said, "Very well, stone her then, but let him who has never sinned cast the first stone."

Of course, one by one, they dropped their stones and vanished into the crowd until only Jesus and the women were left. Jesus asked the women where they had all gone, and she answered that none of the accusers had remained. Jesus responded, "Neither do I condemn you. Go and sin no more."

Here was Jesus stating that although she had sinned that He did not condemn her.

Finally, we have the example of a sexual love affair between a man and a woman recorded in the Song of Solomon. Not only do we have it recorded in the Bible, but we also have it recorded that the women of Jerusalem were encouraging them. We also have no condemnation of their activity anywhere in the Bible. If the Song of Solomon was the only piece of evidence that we could bring to the table, supporting the fact that sex outside of marriage was not sinful or wrong, it would be sufficient as a standalone piece of evidence. But when it stands with all the other evidence that we have looked at, it is without any doubt at all that it is biblical truth. We can also add that there is not one shred of evidence mentioned, or alluded to, anywhere in the Bible that sex outside of marriage is wrong, making the argument absolutely conclusive.

In support of the fact that I believe that it was God's intended intention for humanity to be a matriarchal society, I find my final piece of evidence in the phenomenon of swinging. I want to make it perfectly clear that I am not condoning swinging in any way, shape, or form but simply addressing the issue in regard to my argument regarding matriarchal societies and to state from a biblical perspective that it is not adultery as so many evangelicals claim it to be.

Swinging, as we know it today, was developed on military bases during WWII. Apparently, a group of servicemen and servicewomen got together and worked out an idea that, they believed, would help protect their marriages. They realized that, with the men being gone for so long and with so many eligible young men on the military base, the temptation for their wives to have affairs would be overwhelming. So they formed small groups of couples that they could trust to keep their secret. The plan was that when some men of the group were gone, their wives could have sex with the men who remained in the group. I have absolutely no idea how effective the idea was in protecting their marriages, but I do know that this arrangement was the beginning of what we know today as the swinging culture.

This obviously brings up the question of whether swinging, whereby individuals have sex with other married partners in the group, is adultery. At first glance, it would look like it is, as it involves an individual having sex with someone who is another's spouse.

However, if we take this stance, we need to carefully analyze the concept of adultery. In the Ten Commandments, we have a clear pattern of logic.

The first four commandments given by God in Exodus chapter 20 were in relation to God. The fifth relates to our family, and the remaining five are in relation each other.

- Don't murder.
- Don't commit adultery.
- Don't steal.
- Don't lie in court about your neighbors.
- Don't covet or have an obsession about taking something from your neighbors that belongs to them.

What do these five commandments all have in common? They all are commands concerning actions "against" an individual and about violating your neighbor or their sense of ownership. It has been said that the whole of our present legal system was founded on the right of an individual to protect what was theirs.

So let's take them one at a time.

1. Is murdering someone an act against him/her? Obviously, the answer is yes. Is it taking something from him/her?—again, obviously, yes.
2. Is stealing something an act against a person, and is it an act of taking something from an individual?—again, obviously, yes.
3. Is lying in court about a person something that is done against the defendant, and is it taking something from them? Again, yes.
4. Is obsessing over having something that belongs to someone else against an individual, and will it result in you tak-

ing something from them? Obviously, God thought so, that's why he gave that commandment in order to protect the other four.

All four have the same component of being against an individual and a violation of ownership.

So now let's come to adultery. Does it meet the two criteria? In the first place, God never intended for a couple to own each other. Yes, the concept of a man owning a women came out of the Old Testament but was a result of man's sin. Secondly, if I steal a man's lawn mower, this is clearly forbidden. However, we can agree that if I borrow it from him, there is no problem at all. So even if a man did own a woman, what would be the difference from loaning a lawn mower than loaning a wife or a husband for that matter? That is precisely what Sarah did by loaning her possession, Hagar, to Abraham to have sex with.

It may come as a surprise to many that the concept of a couple loaning out their partner to another for sexual purposes is not entirely new. For the ancient Eskimos, this was part of their culture. When a man visited his friend in another village and needed to stay the night, probably because of adverse weather conditions, it was the normal practice for the host to lend his wife to the guest for the night. This was an arrangement that suited all three.

Once again, because the translation of the Bible is just a translation of words but not a translation of culture, we lose a lot of the intent in the translation due to lack of understanding of another culture. We have already observed that in the context in which this command was given that a woman was a mere possession of the man. There was no assumption of love or commitment that we associate with sexual activity in a martial relationship. The man was free to have sex with any other woman who was not married, and that was not considered adultery.

So the question we have before us is, "Does the couple have a mutual agreement of open relationships with regard to sex?" We must ask the same two questions: Is this an act against someone or against their entitlement of ownership?

If the answer is no in both cases, then it would be clear that open sexual arrangements with the clear consent and support of all concerned would not be adultery.

However, the swinging culture offers some incredible evidence in support of my argument that God's intent was for us to be a matriarchal society. The whole of the swinging culture is organized and run by women. There are also some hardened rules that cannot be broken.

1.  No means no. If a man violates that rule and makes himself a nuisance toward a woman, the women leaders will ask the other men in the group to throw him out.
2.  Swingers not only have group parties but individual couples who are part of the group have sex with other couples when there is no party going on. However, once again, strict rules apply.

Let's say, there are two couples who are members of a swinging group. Let's call them Jack and Jill and Bettie and Bill. If Bill decides one day that he doesn't want to wait for the next party to have sex with Jill, he cannot just call her up and say, "When can we get together?" The rule is that Bill must ask his partner, Bettie, who in turn will call Jill, who will ask Jack. This means that all four are not only in the loop but must approve of the sexual tryst of Bill and Jill.

I often wonder if this is not a lot closer to what God intended than the debacle that we so often have today with couples cheating on each other. The interesting thing to note is that many of the couples involved maintain that their involvement in swinging greatly strengthened their marriages.

Preston Sprinkle and Branson Parlor said the following, "For many Christians, polygamy seems so extreme and rare that there's no need to talk about it. But it is much more common than some people think, and it's growing in popularity. According to one estimate, 'as many as 5 percent of Americans are currently in relationships involving consensual nonmonogamy.' A recent study, published in a peer-reviewed journal, found that 20 percent of Americans have been in a consensual nonmonogamous relationship at least once in their life. Another survey showed that nearly 70 percent of nonreligious Americans between the ages of twenty-four and thirty-five believe that polygamy is okay, even if it's not their cup of tea. And perhaps most shocking of all, according to sociologist Mark Regnerus in *Cheap Sex*, roughly 24 percent of churchgoing people believe that consensual polyamorous relationships are morally permissible."

## Concluding thoughts

In conclusion, we need to go right back to Genesis where I believe we have a very powerful example and message when it comes to the role of women with regard to sexuality. I have already referred to the stories of Abraham and Hagar and Jacob and the two slave girls belonging to Rachael and Leah. In both cases, the husbands had the power of life and death over both their wives and slave girls.

However, there is not even the slightest hint of either of the two men doing anything with the slave girls until, in both cases, their wives gave them to their respective husbands as wives. Here we have a clear biblical example of how godly men are to relate to their wives when it comes to sexuality and the sexual behavior of their husband. The wife is in the driver's seat—end of story.

I will conclude with a statement from Lance Ford written in Christianity Today, "The Hebrew and Greek words for justice are used over one thousand times in the Bible. Compare that to the words for sexual sin, which are used less than one hundred times. Mix these facts with contemporary evangelical and obsession on sexual issues, and you have the epitome of why Jesus would say to the religious, 'Blind guides! You strain your water so that you will not accidentally swallow a gnat, but you swallow a camel' (Matthew 23:25)!

**If we Christians obsessed over justice and mercy like we do over sexuality, we just might change the world."**

I am aware that there are millions of people in the world today who have abandoned their Christian faith because they have been unable to reconcile the teaching of evangelical/fundamentalist/conservative churches with their own convictions regarding Christian sexuality. If you are one of those people, I implore you to come back to the faith that you once had in God through Jesus Christ. You may or may not be able to find a church that is in harmony with your beliefs, but I beg of you not to remain in an estranged relationship with God. Remember, God created sex. It was all his idea.

The reader would have noticed that when it comes to the subject of biblical sexuality, I have said virtually nothing about what the Bible may say, or not say, about homosexuality. I have purposely done this for two reasons. Firstly, it is beyond the scope and purpose of this book.

Secondly, in all honesty, I have been unable to come to any conclusive evidence from scripture on the subject. Yes, I know that things are said, and there are things that are said concerning the interpretation or translation of these things that are said. So for those two reasons, I have not touched on the subject. However, I do feel duty bound to leave you one small piece that I came across as I did research for this book from Gail Labovitz from the Tannaitic Midrash, "There is no direct prohibition on female homoerotic sexual activity in the Hebrew Bible, indeed, no explicit discussion of such activity at all. Biblical laws of forbidden sexual couplings (notably Leviticus chapter 18 and 20) are generally addressed to male listeners/readers. With the exception of the prohibition against bestiality (Leviticus 18:23 and 20:15–16) in which the prohibition against women committing this act follows on the prohibition to men, sexual acts which do not involve male participants are not discussed."

The end.

# BIBLIOGRAPHY


Ahlgrim, Ryan. Pastor of the First Mennonite Church in Richmond Virginia posted on his blog.

Amrosino, Brandon. British Broadcasting Corporation Future.

Anderton, J. T. "The Red Pill Bible Guy." "Will Pastors Marry Couples Living Together?" www.rosewoodandolive.com.

Bolzer-Weber, Nadia. *Shameless: A Sexual Revolution.* Convergent Books, an imprint of the Crown Publishing Group, division of Penguin Random House LLC New York, page 190. Copyright 2019.

Bulwer. "History of Athens," chap. 6.

Carmichael, James. "Israeli Special Forces and Intelligence Services." Copyright 2017.

Dr. Howel, Kenneth. www.catholic.com/magazine/print-edition/how-can-you-say-that-mary-is-the-new-eve.

Ford, Lance. "Christianity Today."

Freedman, David. "The Biblical Archaeology Review." www.god-sword to women. Sulik. References R. and 9 [1983]: 56–58.

Gaddini, Katie. "A Large Number of Single Women Are Leaving the Church. Why?" revelvantmagazine.com.

Gruber, Tom. Martin Luther. Christianstalking aboutSex.com.

Hannah. "Will Pastors Marry Couples Living Together?" www.rosewoodandolive.com.

Hinkley, Chesna. CBE International. Published June 13, 2019.

Hogenboom, Melissa. British Broadcasting Corporation Earth.

Instone-Brewer, David. Blog, "Premier Christianity." Why Christians Should Ditch the Idea of Original Sin, October 28, 2021.

Labovitz, Gail, Rabbi Senior Research Analyst, Female Homoerotic Sexual Activity-American Jewish University. Source. "Tannaitic Midrash."

Lim, Israel, C. S. "Patriarchy Website-History of Manogamy-Catholic Priests Were Monogamous and Polygamous but Made Celibate." Copyright July 1998.

Mowczko, Marg. Blog August 1, 2019.

Mowczko, Marg. "Wiliaming: The Biblical Theology of Christian Egalitarianism-Equality in Marriage-Head and Source." Blog July 22, 2017. Exploringgod'swordtowomen.org/ezerkenegdo.

Native American website ya-native.com.

Nye, Joseph, Jr. "The Future of Power." Published in the United States by Public affairs TM, a member of the Perseus Books Group. Copyright 2011, all rights reserved.

Ogden, Lesley Evans. Blog "What the Animals Teach us about Female Leadership."

Preston, Sprinkle and Parlor Branson. "Christianity Today," Feb 2020.

Rabbi Lerner, Michael. "The Left Hand of God-Taking Our Country Back from the Religious Right." Publisher Harper San Francisco.

Rich, Tracey R. Blog, "Kosher Sex, Level: Intermediate."

Sexuality in the Middle Ages—See U in History/Mythology. Published June 10, 2021.

"The Week" Written by the staff, "The Origins of Marriage" January 1, 2007.

Troy, Charles. "The Christian Left" Blog-Premarital Sex: Is It a Sin or Not. November 19, 2013.

Wilson and Reeder. "Mammal Species of the World" 3rd Edition. Published by Johns Hopkins University Press.

Wood, Hannelie. Department of Philosophy and Systematic Theology, University of South Africa. "Feminists and Their Perspectives on Church Fathers Regarding Women."

# ABOUT THE AUTHOR

Dean Robertson is a retired evangelical minister. He has spent his entire adult life in Christian ministry in various capacities, including senior pastor, church planter, mission director, evangelist, denominational superintendent, and keynote convention speaker. He is also a studious biblical scholar. He has a master's degree in intercultural studies, and his international ministry has taken him to many areas of the world.

He can be contacted via email at <deanrobertsonbooks@gmail.com>